decorating glass

decorating glass

add colour to your home with
beautiful hand-painted decorations
and exciting mosaic projects

michael ball

southwater

Publisher's Note

Protective clothing should be worn
when performing certain tasks
described in this book. Wear rubber
(latex) gloves for grouting, using
glass etching paste and cleaning
with hydrochloric acid; wear leather
gloves when breaking mosaic
tesserae with a hammer; wear
goggles when breaking tesserae
with a hammer, using tile nippers
and cleaning with hydrochloric acid;
wear a face mask when sanding,
cleaning with hydrochloric acid,
cleaning lead with a wire (steel)
brush and working with the
following: powdered grout, cement,
sprays (such as adhesive or varnish)
and lead came.

Acknowledgements

The publishers would like to thank the
following people for designing and
making projects in this book:
Helen Baird for the Jazzy Plant Pot,
Mosaic Bottle, Country Cottage Tray,
Mosaic Table and Garden Urn.
Michael Ball for the Lemonade
Pitcher, Alhambra Picture Frame, Folk
Art Cabinet, Lily Candle Bowl, Banded
Vase, Door Number Plaque, Opal
Glass Planter, Cherry Blossom Vase
and Window Hanging. **Emma Biggs**
for the Abstract Mirror. **Petra Boase**
for the Frosted Vase. **Tessa Brown** for
the Love Letter Rack. **Anna-Lise
De'Ath** for the Sunlight Catcher,
Patterned Bathroom Bottle, Leaded
Picture Frames, Leaded Door Panels
and Mosaic Lantern. **Mary Fellows**
for the Geometric Bordered Frame
and Stained-glass Window. **Lucinda
Ganderton** for the Venetian Perfume
Bottle, Leaf Photograph Frame,
Bohemian Bottle and French-lavender
Flower Vase. **Sandra Hadfield** for the
Door Number Plaque and Mosaic Fire
Screen. **Susie Johns** for the Christmas
Baubles. **Emma Micklethwaite** for
the Bathroom Cabinet Door Panel.
Joanna Nevin for the Stained-glass
Screen. **Deirdre O'Malley** for the
Indoor Glass Lantern and Curtain
Decorations. **Cheryl Owen** for the
Champagne Flutes. **Polly Plouviez** for
the Glass Nugget Bottle Holder.
Debbie Siniska for the Heart Light
Catcher. **Isabel Stanley** for the Fish
Splashback. **Norma Vondee** for the
Aztec Box. **Stewart Walton** for the
Folk Art Glass.

Contents

Introduction

Decorating glass is absorbing and satisfying and produces beautiful results. Painting glass is the easiest craft to start. You can transform glassware

with an assortment of colourful patterns, and a

variety of paint techniques. Combining glass painting with strips of lead came creates the look of stained glass and is a lovely way to decorate lanterns, window hangings and even door panels. Glass mosaic is another skill that makes the most of the translucent quality of coloured glass.

As well as illustrating all the different techniques involved in decorating glass, this book contains over 40 step-by-step projects ranging from simple to complex and from small to large. If you want to start with glass painting, you can try champagne flutes decorated with simple fizzing bubbles, and progress on to a candle bowl decorated with an attractive pattern of painted water lilies. The chapter on stained glass includes a heart light catcher and other simple projects, as

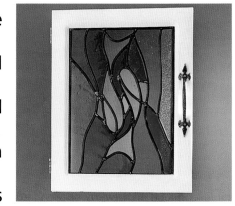

well as more ambitious ideas, such as a bathroom cabinet door panel. In the chapter on glass mosaic you can choose between a love letter rack or jazzy plant pot to start with and progress on to a mosaic tabletop or even a garden urn. The symbol ∤ indicates that a project is relatively straightforward to do and that a complete beginner could tackle it with ease. Projects with the symbol ∤∤∤∤∤ indicate that an advanced level of skill and knowledge is required.

If you are artistic you may want to design your own patterns for painting

or for your mosaic, but if not there are plenty of templates at the back of the book. Some of the simplest designs can be the most effective, especially when colour is the most important element of the design. For example, contrasting lines or blocks of colour painted around a drinking glass or vase can look very striking. Stained glass also works best with simple shapes and bold designs. Likewise with glass mosaic; using simple gradations of colour rather than a complicated design allows the colours to shine

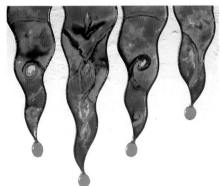

through. Remember that it is always best to practise first on spare glassware before undertaking a project. This will give you the confidence to complete your project with ease.

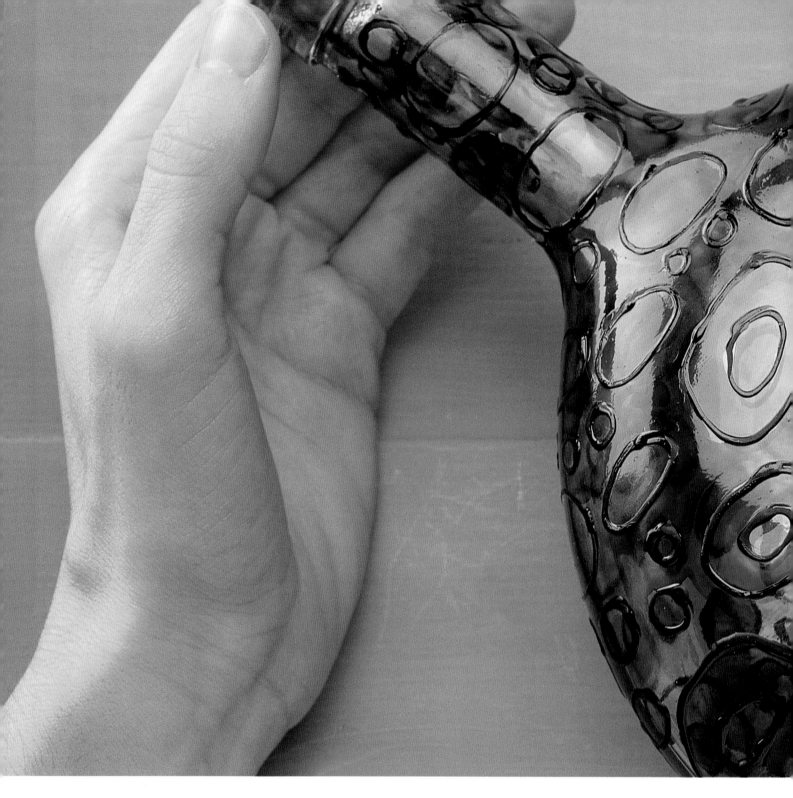

Decorating

Glass

In recent years a wide range of glass paints, in a glorious array of colours, has been made available to the amateur. These paints do not require kiln firing to set them, and can be applied easily to glassware. So whether you want to recreate the effect of a stained-glass window in your home, or add delicate colour to perfume bottles and champagne flutes to celebrate a special occasion, there are plenty of ideas here to inspire you.

Decorative Details

Glass painting allows you to transform everyday glass bottles, jars, vases, frames, mirrors and even windows into works of art in glorious jewel colours and decorative patterns. All you need are some glass paints, paintbrushes and some glassware to decorate. No specialist skills are required, just a love of colour.

To start with, you can use empty glass bottles and jars salvaged from the kitchen and bathroom to practise on. Then, as you become more proficient and confident, you can progress to decorating plain glass vases, storage jars, perfume bottles, frames,

bowls and even mirrors. You can paint simple dots and squiggles on wine glasses and Christmas baubles, add colourful butterflies and flowers around the outside of glass bowls, decorate jars and frames with charming folk-art

patterns, or perhaps paint trails of pretty flower tendrils across small windows or mirrors.

In addition to painting motifs and patterns, you could try your hand at paint effects on glass, such as sponging, dragging, or scribing with a toothpick.

All of these techniques are clearly explained at the beginning of the chapter with illustrated step-by-step instructions.

Contour paste adds further possibilities to painting glass. It can be used to outline areas, preventing different colours from merging and blending, or to add raised decorative lines on top of a painted area. Squares of different coloured contour pastes can provide decoration in themselves, without the use of glass paints.

The projects in this chapter feature a variety of different ideas and styles of painting to inspire you, from a colourful geometric frame for your

favourite picture, to a frosted vase to add interest to a windowsill. Templates and motifs for many of them can be found at the back of the book, enabling you to transfer the designs exactly. Other projects allow you to experiment with freehand painting, so you can introduce some individual elements into the design. After all, if you make a mistake – you can simply wipe it away.

A variety of materials is needed for painting glass including glass paints and etching paste, available from specialist glass shops, and self-adhesive vinyl, which is available from craft shops.

Materials

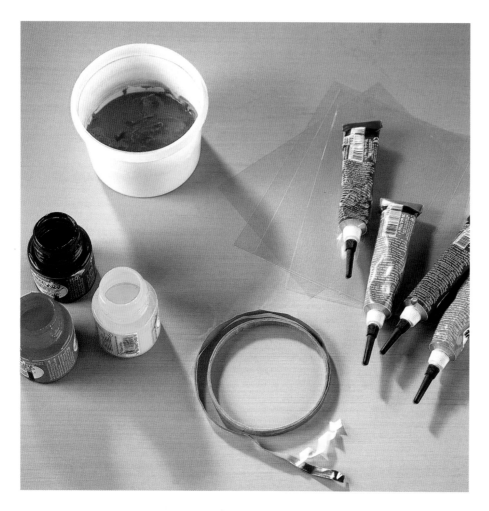

colour. They are not washable, and are designed purely for decorative use. Oil-based and water-based glass paints are available: the two types should not be combined. Ceramic paints can also be used on glass for an opaque effect.

Masking tape

This is ideal for making straight lines for etching and painting.

Paper towels

These are useful for cleaning glass and brushes, and wiping off mistakes.

Reusable adhesive

This is useful for holding designs in place on the glass.

Self-adhesive vinyl

Vinyl is used to mask off large areas when painting and etching the glass.

Acrylic enamel paints

These are ideal for use on glass.

Clear varnish

Mix with glass paints to produce lighter hues.

Contour paste

Use to create raised lines on glass. This gives the look of leaded windows and also acts as a barrier for paints. It can be used to add details within a cell of colour, such as the veins on a leaf.

Epoxy glue

Use this strong, clear glue to attach hanging devices to glass. It takes just a few minutes to go hard.

Etching paste

This acid paste eats into the surface of glass to leave a matt "frosted" finish. Use on clear and pale-coloured glass.

Glass paints

Specially manufactured, glass paints are translucent and give a vibrant

Toothpicks

Use to scratch designs into paintwork.

Ultraviolet glue

This glue goes hard in daylight. Red glass blocks ultraviolet rays, so you should let the light shine through the non-red glass when sticking two colours together, or use epoxy glue.

White spirit (paint thinner)

Use as a solvent to clean off most paints and any errors.

A well-lit workplace and a paintbrush are all that are needed for many of the projects in this chapter. However, the items listed below will make the job easier.

Equipment

Paintbrushes
Use a selection of artist's paintbrushes for applying paint and etching paste. Always clean brushes as directed by the paint manufacturer.

Paint palette
Large quantities of glass paint can be mixed in a plastic ice-cube tray.

Pencils and pens
Use a pencil or dark-coloured felt-tipped pen when making templates. A chinagraph can be used to draw guide-lines on the glass and wipes off easily.

Rubber (latex) gloves
A pair of gloves is vital to protect your hands from etching paste.

Ruler or straightedge
These are essential for measuring, or when a straight line is needed.

Scissors
A pair of small, sharp scissors is useful for various cutting tasks, including cutting out templates.

Sponges
Cut sponges into pieces and use them to apply paint over a large area of glass. A natural sponge can be used to give the paint a decorative mottled effect, whereas a synthetic sponge will give a more regular effect.

Cloth
A piece of cloth or towel folded into a pad is useful to provide support for items such as bottles or bowls while they are being painted. Paint one side of a vessel first, then allow it to dry thoroughly before resting it on the cloth while you paint the rest.

Cotton buds (swabs)
Use these to wipe away any painted mistakes and to remove chinagraph pencil marks.

Craft knife
A craft knife is useful for peeling off contour paste in glass-painting and etching projects. Ensure the blade is sharp and clean.

Nail polish remover
Before painting, always clean the glass on both sides to remove all traces of grease or fingerprints. Household glass-cleaning products can be used but nail polish remover is just as good. Use with paper towels.

On the following pages you will find useful step-by-step descriptions of some of the basic glass-painting techniques. They will help you to perfect your skills and achieve beautiful and successful results.

Techniques

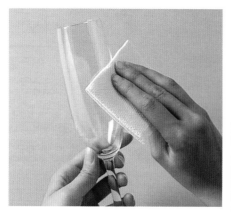

Preparing the glass

It is essential to clean the surface of the glass thoroughly to remove any traces of grease or fingermarks, before beginning glass painting.

Clean both sides of the glass thoroughly, using a glass cleaner or nail polish remover and a paper towel.

Using templates and stencils

There are many different templates and stencils suitable for using on glass. Choose the type that is most useful for the size and style of glassware you are decorating.

1 If you are working on a flat piece of clear glass, a template can simply be taped to the underside or attached using pieces of reusable putty adhesive, to ensure it does not move.

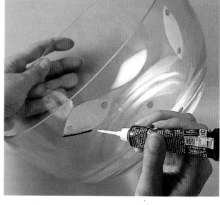

2 When you are decorating a curved surface, such as a bowl, small paper templates can be attached to the inside, following the curve. Use adhesive tape.

3 When working on a small, curved surface, such as a drinking glass, it may be easier to apply the template to the outside and then draw around it using a chinagraph pencil to make a guide.

4 Cut straight-sided stencils using a craft knife and metal ruler and resting on a cutting mat. Always keep your fingers well away from the blade and change the blade frequently to avoid tearing the paper.

5 When you are cutting a stencil that includes tight curves, cut what you can with a craft knife, then use a small pair of sharp-pointed scissors to cut the curves smoothly.

Transferring a design

In addition to using templates and stencils, there are several other ways of transferring a design on to glass. You can trace it, sketch with a pen, use carbon paper or even use water.

Tracing through the glass

Stick the design in position on the back of the article you wish to transfer it to with reusable putty adhesive or masking tape. For curved vessels cut the design into sections. Trace the design directly on to the surface of the vessel with the tube of contour paste.

Felt-tipped pens

A water-based overhead-projection pen is ideal for sketching freehand on to glass. Many felt-tipped pens will also work. When you are happy with your design, apply contour paste over the lines.

Water-level technique

To draw even lines around a vase, bowl, or other circular vessel, fill with water to the height of the line. Turn the vessel slowly while tracing the waterline on to the surface of the glass with contour paste.

Using carbon paper

Place a sheet of carbon paper over the article and then put the design on top. With a ballpoint pen, trace over the lines of your design, pressing it fairly firmly. Some carbon papers will not work on glass – handwriting carbon paper is the most suitable.

Using contour paste

Contour paste is easy to use, but it takes a little practice to get the pressure right. As it is the basis of much glass painting, it is worth persevering.

1 Squeeze the tube until the paste just begins to come out, then stop. To draw a line, hold the tube at about 45° to the surface. Rest the tip of the tube on the glass and squeeze it gently while moving the tube.

2 Occasionally air bubbles occur inside the tube. These can cause the paste to "explode" out of the tube. If this happens, either wipe off the excess paste straight away with a paper towel, or wait until it has dried and use a craft knife to remove it.

Mixing and applying paint

Glass paints come in a range of exciting, vivid colours, and produce beautiful translucent effects. Practise painting first on a spare piece of glass to get used to the consistency of the paint.

1 Mix paint colours on a ceramic palette, old plate or tile. To make a light colour, add the colour to white or colourless paint, a tiny amount at a time, until you reach the required hue. Use a separate brush for each colour so that you do not contaminate the paint in the pot.

2 If you want the finished effect to be opaque rather than translucent, add a small amount of white glass paint to the transparent coloured paint on the palette, plate or tile.

3 Always use an appropriately sized paintbrush for the job. A large, flat brush will give a smooth and even coverage over larger areas of glass, as well as making the job quicker.

4 Use a very fine brush to paint small details and fine lines. Let one coat of paint dry before painting over it with another colour.

5 To etch a design into the paint, draw into the paint while it is still wet using a toothpick or the other end of the paintbrush. Wipe off the excess paint after each stroke to keep the design clean.

Applying paint with a sponge

Sponging produces a mottled, softened effect on glass surfaces. Experiment first on scrap paper.

1 Use a dampened natural sponge to achieve a mottled effect. Dip the sponge in the paint then blot it on a sheet of paper to remove the excess paint before applying it to the glass.

2 Use masking tape or small pieces of reusable putty adhesive to attach the stencil to the glass for sponging.

Free-styling

Rather than using contour paste to define individual cells of colour, apply a coat of varnish over the article and brush or drop colours into the varnish, allowing them to blend freely.

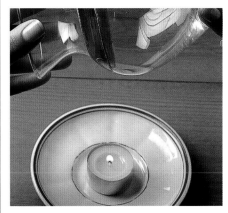

3 Add texture and interest to sponged decoration by adding a second colour when the first has dried. This is most effective when both sides of the glass will be visible.

4 Sponge a neat, decorative band around a drinking glass by masking off both sides of the band with strips of masking tape.

Flash drying with candles

It is possible to flash dry paintwork over a heat source. A candle is ideal, but take care not to burn yourself. Turn the article slowly about 15cm/ 6in above the flame.

Correcting mistakes

If you don't get your design right first time, it doesn't matter with glass painting. All you need is a cotton bud (swab) or a paper towel and you can simply wipe off the paint before it dries.

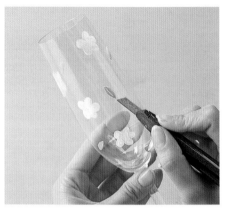

1 Use a cotton bud (swab) to remove a small mistake. Work while the paint is still wet.

2 To remove a larger area of paint, wipe it away immediately using a damp paper towel. If the paint has begun to dry, use nail polish remover.

3 If the paint has hardened completely, small mistakes can be corrected by scraping the paint away using a craft knife.

Etching glass

This technique is easy but very effective and produces a quick, stylish finish. Etch simple shapes such as flowers or leaves for the best results.

1 Self-adhesive vinyl makes a good mask when etching. Cut out shapes from self-adhesive vinyl. Decide where you want to position them on the glass, remove the backing paper and stick down.

2 Wearing rubber (latex) gloves, paint the etching paste evenly over the glass with a paintbrush. Make sure you do not spread it too thinly, or you will find the effect quite faint. Leave to dry for 3 minutes.

3 Still wearing the rubber gloves, wash the paste off with running water. Then wipe off any residue and rinse. Peel off the shapes and wash again. Dry the glass thoroughly with a clean cotton rag.

For this year's Christmas tree, buy plain glass baubles and decorate them yourself with coloured glass paints to make beautiful, completely original ornaments.

Christmas Baubles

You will need

self-adhesive spots

clean, clear glass baubles

glass etching medium

paper clips

gold contour paste

fine glitter

scrap paper

bright yellow glass paint

fine artist's paintbrush

1 Stick self-adhesive spots all over the baubles. Spray on an even coat of glass etching medium. Hang up each bauble to dry using paper clips.

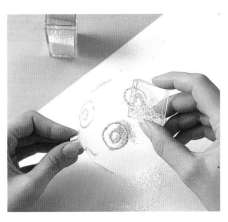

2 Peel off the paper spots to reveal clear circles all over each bauble. Outline each circle with gold contour paste, then draw a second circle around the first. Add some squiggly lines radiating from the neck of the bauble. While the contour paste is still wet, sprinkle it with glitter, holding the bauble over a sheet of paper to catch the excess. Hang the bauble up to dry.

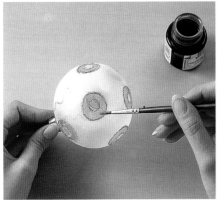

3 Fill in between the inner and outer gold circles with glass paint in bright yellow, and hang the bauble up to dry, using paper clips as before. Repeat for any remaining baubles.

The decoration on this double-layered glass frame has been painted on to the inside of the glass. This means that you need to paint the details on the leaves first, and the background colour second.

Leaf Photograph Frame

You will need
tracing paper
double-layer glass clip-frame, with cleaned glass
scissors
masking tape
photograph
felt-tipped pen
nail polish remover or glass cleaner
paper towels
fine and medium artist's paintbrushes
glass paints: dark green, light green and pale blue

1 Cut a piece of tracing paper the same size as the frame. Using small tabs of masking tape, stick your chosen photograph in place and mark its position, then draw a selection of leaves around it, following the leaf templates at the back of the book.

2 Thoroughly clean the glass that forms the front of the frame. Remove the photograph and turn the tracing paper back to front. Attach it to the glass using small pieces of masking tape, as shown.

3 Using a fine paintbrush, fill in the leaf stems of the design with the dark green paint. Again using the dark green paint, fill in the small triangle shapes that represent the veins in the leaves. Leave the dark green paint to dry completely.

4 Paint the leaf shapes in light green. Leave the light green paint to dry, then paint the background colour in pale blue. Leave to dry. Remove the template. Bake the glass frame to harden the paint, if necessary. Follow the manufacturer's instructions.

5 Attach your chosen photograph to the second glass sheet, checking its position against the marks on the template. Assemble the frame.

Stained glass is made for sunlight, and this sunlight catcher can hang in any window to catch all of the available light. Gold outliner separates the brightly coloured areas of orange, yellow, red and blue.

Sunlight Catcher

You will need

clean, 20cm/8in diameter clear glass roundel, 4mm/³⁄₁₆in thick

paper

pencil

tracing paper

indelible black felt-tipped pen

gold contour paste

glass paints: orange, yellow, red and blue

fine artist's paintbrush

73cm/29in length of chain

pliers

epoxy glue

1 To make a template of the sun motif that will fit the glass roundel, start by using a pencil to draw around the rim of the roundel on to a piece of paper.

2 Trace the sun motif template from the back of the book and transfer it to the plain paper, enlarging to the size required.

4 Trace over the black lines using gold contour paste. Leave to dry.

5 Colour in the central sun motif using the orange and yellow glass paints. Leave to dry. Clean the brush between colours as recommended by the paint manufacturer.

3 Place the circle of glass over the template and trace the design on to the glass using a felt-tipped pen.

6 Fill in the rest of the design using red and blue glass paints. Leave to dry.

7 Wrap the length of chain around the edge of the glass and cut to size. Rejoin the links by squeezing firmly together with pliers.

8 Cut an 8cm/3¼in length of chain, open the links at each end, and attach it to the chain circle by squeezing with pliers. Glue the chain circle around the circumference of the glass roundel using epoxy glue.

Get into the spirit of summer with this unusual etched lemonade pitcher. Etching is particularly suitable for eating or drinking vessels as once the piece has been washed there is no surface residue.

Lemonade Pitcher

You will need

clean glass pitcher

tape measure

tracing paper

pencil

scissors

reusable putty adhesive

black contour paste

self-adhesive vinyl or PVA (white) glue
and brush

etching paste

1cm/½in decorator's paintbrush

washing up (dishwashing) brush

craft knife

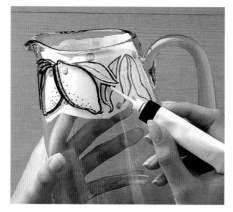

1 Measure the top rim of the pitcher. Trace and enlarge the template at the back of the book to fit. Cut into sections and space evenly inside the pitcher, just below the neck. Trace the design on to the glass with the contour paste. Leave to dry for 2 hours.

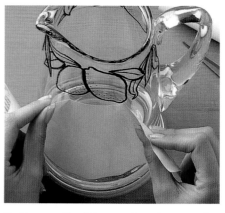

2 Cover all of the pitcher (except the design area) with self-adhesive vinyl or two costs of PVA (white) glue. If using glue, leave the first coat to dry completely before applying the next.

3 Fill in all of the gaps between the outlines of the lemons and leaves and the vinyl (or glue) with black contour paste. Apply the etching paste with the decorator's paintbrush following the manufacturer's instructions.

4 Wash off the etching paste with cold water. If the etching paste has done its job, the glass should now be evenly etched without clear patches or streaks, but if it does not seem quite right, reapply the etching paste.

5 Carefully lift the edge of the contour paste with a craft knife. Peel off the vinyl (if used) and the contour paste. The paste will peel off more easily if you warm the pitcher by wrapping it in a hot towel first.

This picture frame is simply decorated using a gold marker and glass paints. The design is inspired by the devotional art and the remarkable patterns that adorn the Alhambra Palace in Granada, southern Spain.

Alhambra Picture Frame

You will need

clip-frame, with cleaned glass

gold permanent felt-tipped pen

fine artist's paintbrush

glass paints: crimson, turquoise and deep blue

piece of glass

scissors

kitchen sponge

paper towel

1 Enlarge the template at the back of the book to fit the clip-frame. Remove the glass from the frame and place it over the design. Trace it on to the glass with a gold permanent felt-tipped pen.

2 Turn the sheet of glass over. Using a fine paintbrush, paint over the diamond shapes with the crimson glass paints. Leave a white border between the crimson and the gold outline.

3 Pour a little turquoise and a little deep blue paint on to a piece of glass. Cut a kitchen sponge into sections. Press the sponge into the paint and then apply it to the glass with a light, dabbing motion to colour in the border. Clean up any overspill with a paper towel and leave to dry.

This is a magical way to transform a plain glass vase into something stylish and utterly original. When you have etched the vase, make sure that it is evenly frosted before you peel off the leaves.

Frosted Vase

You will need

coloured glass vase

tracing paper

pencil

thin cardboard or paper

scissors

self-adhesive vinyl

etching paste

medium artist's paintbrush

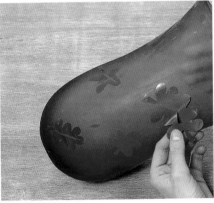

1 Wash and dry the vase. Draw a leaf pattern, then trace it on to a piece of thin cardboard or paper. Cut them out. Draw around the templates on to the backing of the vinyl and draw small circles freehand.

2 Cut out the shapes and peel off the backing paper. Arrange the shapes all over the vase. Smooth them down carefully to avoid any wrinkles. Paint etching paste over the vase and leave it in a warm place to dry, following the manufacturer's instructions.

3 Wash the vase in warm water to remove the paste. If the frosting looks smooth, you can remove the shapes. If not, repeat the process with another coat of etching paste, then wash and remove the shapes.

This jazzy painted bottle will really brighten up a bathroom shelf. It is decorated with a fun bubble pattern in blues and greens, but you can experiment with designs to complement the shape of your bottle.

Patterned Bathroom Bottle

You will need

clean glass bottle with a cork

felt-tipped pen

paper

black contour paste

glass paints: blue, green, violet and turquoise

fine artist's paintbrushes

ultraviolet glue

turquoise glass nugget

bubble bath

1 Decide on the pattern you think would look best for your bottle, then sketch your design to scale on a piece of paper.

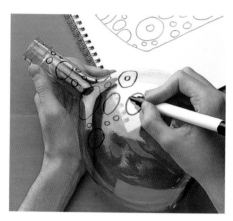

2 Wash and thoroughly dry the bottle you have chosen. Then, using a felt-tipped pen, copy your design carefully on to the bottle.

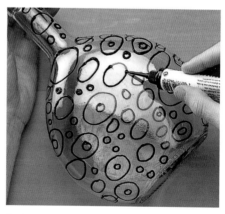

3 Trace the felt-tipped pen design on one side of the bottle with the black contour paste. Leave the contour paste to dry completely.

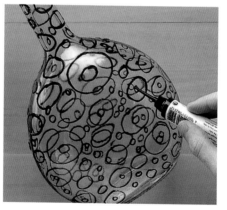

4 Turn the bottle over and add contour paste circles to the other side. Leave to dry as before.

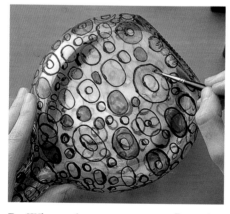

5 When the contour paste is dry, paint inside the circle motifs using blue, green and violet glass paints. Clean all the paintbrushes thoroughly between colours, as recommended by the paint manufacturer.

6 Once the circles are dry, paint the surrounding area using turquoise glass paint. Leave to dry.

7 Using ultraviolet glue, stick a glass nugget to the top of the cork.

8 Fill the bottle with your favourite bubble bath and replace the cork.

Celebratory champagne bubbles were the inspiration for these gold-spotted glasses. A fine mist of white paint is applied with a sponge. This is accentuated with a raised design of gold bubbles.

Champagne Flutes

You will need

clean, clear glass champagne flutes

nail polish remover or glass cleaner

paper towels

flat paintbrush

white glass paint

ceramic tile or old plate

natural sponge

water or white spirit (paint thinner)

scrap paper

felt-tipped pen

gold contour paste

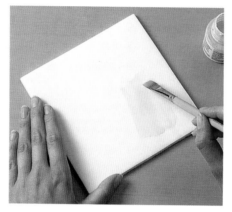

1 Clean the champagne glasses carefully to remove any traces of grease and fingermarks. Using a flat paintbrush, apply a thin film of white glass paint over the surface of a ceramic tile or an old plate.

2 Moisten a piece of natural sponge, using water if the glass paint is water-based or white spirit (paint thinner) if it is oil-based. Dab the sponge on to the paint on the tile or plate.

3 Sponge white paint lightly on to the base, the stem and the lower part of the bowl of each champagne flute. Leave to dry thoroughly. Draw around the base of one glass on a small piece of scrap paper to make a template.

4 Fold the template into eighths, open it out and draw along the fold lines with a pen. Stand the glass on the template and dot along the guide-lines using a gold contour paste. Add dots in a gradual spiral around the glass stem, turning the glass slowly and working upwards.

5 Add more dots on the bowl of the glass, making the dots smaller and placing them further apart as you work up the glass. Place the final dots 2.5cm/1in below the rim so that they do not come in contact with the lips. Repeat with the other glasses. Set the paint following the paint manufacturer's instructions.

Cheap clip-frames are widely available in almost any size you need. This one is decorated with contour paste in a range of colours which have been dragged together while still wet to create an intricate design.

Geometric Bordered Frame

You will need

clip-frame

scrap paper

felt-tipped pen

ruler

nail polish remover or glass cleaner

paper towels

reusable putty adhesive

contour paste: yellow, bright pink, green and orange

toothpick

1 Dismantle the frame and place the glass on a sheet of scrap paper. Draw around the edge of the glass.

2 Divide the marked edge equally and draw a double border of squares around the template.

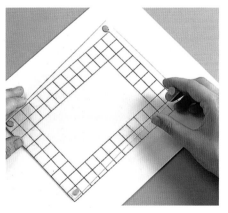

3 Clean the glass thoroughly to remove any traces of grease. Attach the cleaned glass to the paper template with a small piece of reusable putty adhesive at each of the corners.

4 Using yellow contour paste, trace around the first square very carefully, drawing just inside the guidelines of the paper template.

5 Using the bright pink contour paste, draw a slightly smaller square just inside the yellow one. Make sure the two colours meet up exactly without any gap.

6 Draw a third line in the same way using green contour paste. Draw carefully to avoid smudging the yellow and pink paste.

7 Fill the centre of the square with the orange contour paste. Work in single strokes to prevent the orange and green paints from blending.

8 Working while the paste is still wet, use a toothpick to drag the colours from the corners of the square into the centre. Clean the excess paint from the toothpick with a paper towel after each stroke to keep the design neat.

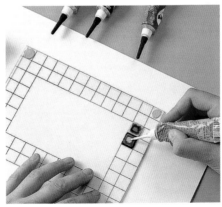

9 Drag another line from the middle of each side of the square into the centre. Wipe the toothpick after each stroke. Repeat on the next square: this time start with green, then use orange, pink and finally yellow in the centre.

10 Work all around the border of the frame, alternating the combinations of colours. Leave the frame to dry completely. Bake the glass to harden the paint, if necessary, following the manufacturer's instructions.

Filled with water and floating candles, this bowl becomes a magical item. Set it on the dining table with the bowl as a centrepiece, or place it in the bathroom, fill the bath, sit back and relax.

Lily Candle Bowl

You will need

masking tape

clean glass bowl

tracing paper

felt-tipped pen

scissors

reusable putty adhesive

black contour paste

glass paints: emerald, deep blue, turquoise, yellow and white

clear varnish

paint palette

fine artist's paintbrushes

piece of glass

washing-up (dishwashing) sponge

cotton buds (swabs)

white spirit (paint thinner)

craft knife

1 Stick masking tape around the rim of the bowl. Trace the template from the back of the book, enlarge it and cut it into small sections. Attach it to the inside of the bowl with reusable putty adhesive. On the outside of the bowl, trace over the design with black contour paste. Complete one half of the bowl, leave it to dry, then do the other half. Draw wavy lines with black contour paste across the bowl between the lily-pads. Leave to dry.

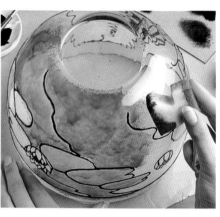

2 Mix one part of emerald glass paint with one part varnish in a container. Repeat with the blue, turquoise and yellow paints. Use a brush to transfer the paint on to a piece of glass. Cut a washing-up (dishwashing) sponge into sections, one piece for each colour. Place the bowl upside down and sponge the turquoise and deep blue over the background. Then sponge emerald and yellow over each lily-pad. Leave to dry for 1–2 hours.

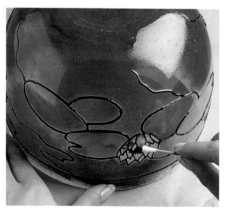

3 Dip a cotton bud (swab) in white spirit (paint thinner) and use it to clean the coloured paint from the flower petals.

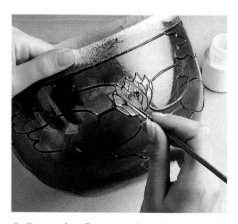

4 Paint the flowers white. Use a craft knife to peel off the contour paste from around the lily-pads, leaving the paste around the flowers intact.

Stems of French lavender, with their picturesque winged flowerheads, criss-cross over the front of this beautiful vase. Opaque paints give the flowers solidity and impact against the clear glass.

French-lavender Flower Vase

You will need
tracing paper
felt-tipped pen
straight-sided glass vase
scissors
masking tape
nail polish remover or glass cleaner
paper towels
high-density synthetic sponge
opaque ceramic paints: gold, white,
purple, crimson and green
paint palette
medium and fine artist's paintbrushes

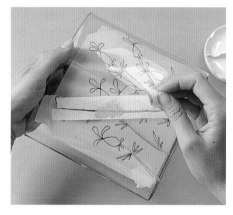

1 Trace the template at the back of the book, enlarging it as necessary to fit the vase. Using masking tape, attach the tracing to the inside of the glass. Clean the outside of the vase thoroughly to remove any traces of grease and fingermarks.

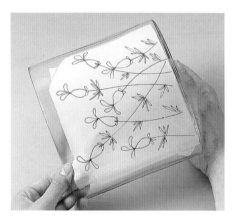

2 Draw a shallow curve along a length of masking tape and cut along it. Stick the two parts to the vase, following one of the stems on the template and leaving a 3mm/⅛in space between them. Sponge gold paint along the stem and leave to dry. Peel off the tape and repeat for the other stems.

3 Mix white with purple paint and fill in the teardrop shapes for the flowerheads in light purple. Add darker shades of purple and crimson towards the bottom end of each flower shape, stippling the paint to create texture.

4 Paint the three petals at the top of each flower in pale purple, using long, loose brush strokes. Leave the paint to dry. Indicate the individual florets on each flowerhead with small ovals in dark purple. Leave the paint to dry.

5 Using a fine paintbrush, draw spiky leaves along the stems in two or three shades of dusky green. Leave to dry completely, and then bake the vase to harden the paint if necessary, following the manufacturer's instructions.

Some bottles are too beautiful to discard. This elegantly shaped blue one has been recycled with a decoration inspired by a 19th-century original found in an antique shop.

Bohemian Bottle

You will need
tracing paper
pencil
scissors
blue bottle
nail polish remover or glass cleaner
paper towels
masking tape
chinagraph pencil
ceramic paints: gold, white, green, red and yellow
medium and fine artist's paintbrushes
paint palette

1 Trace the template at the back of the book and cut out the bold centre section. Clean the bottle to remove any grease and fingermarks. Tape the template to the bottle and draw all around it using a chinagraph pencil.

2 Fill in the shape with several coats of gold paint, stippling it on to create a textured effect. Leave the paint to dry. Using white paint and a fine brush, outline the shape and add swirls along the top edge.

3 Mix white with a little green paint and shade the border design with touches of pale green.

4 Paint the green leaves with loose brush strokes, and add highlights in pale green. Draw in the red and yellow dots along the curves of the border as well as for the flower centres.

5 Paint in the daisy petals around the red flower centres using white paint. Add three small hearts and one or two small yellow flowers to the design for decorative detail.

Painted glassware was a popular folk art form in Europe, with bright figures used to adorn glass, wood, fabric and ceramics. Try to find old glasses in junk or antique shops to decorate.

Folk Art Glass

You will need
tape measure
clean, tall glass
scissors
tracing paper
pencil
masking tape (optional)
soft cloth
enamel paint thinners
enamel paints: red, green, yellow, blue, black and white
fine artist's paintbrushes
elastic band

1 Measure around your glass, top and bottom, and cut a piece of tracing paper to fit in it. Trace the template from the back of the book and put the tracing into the glass, using the masking tape to secure it, if necessary.

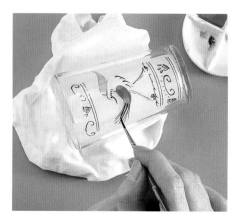

2 Rest the glass on a cloth. Support your painting hand with your other hand. The enamel paint should be thinned just enough to flow nicely and be slightly transparent. Use light strokes and avoid overpainting.

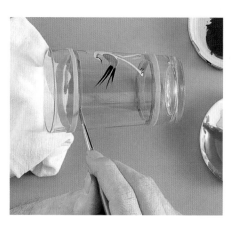

3 When the paint has dried, place an elastic band around the glass to act as a guide, and then paint stripes of colour around it, as shown. Support the glass with a cloth and your other hand, as described in step 2.

4 Add small motifs to suit your glass; if you have a fluted base, emphasize this with a pattern. Allow one side of the glass to dry first before painting the other, unless you support the glass on its rim by splaying your other hand inside the glass.

5 Finally, introduce some individual touches by adding embellishments of your own to the design, perhaps in the form of just a few squiggles, some dots or even your initials.

This enchanting perfume bottle, with its swags of little dots and pretty little gilded flowers, is reminiscent of 19th-century Italian enamelled glassware. Use opaque ceramic paints for this project.

Venetian Perfume Bottle

You will need

round clear glass bottle with stopper
nail polish remover or glass cleaner
paper towels
tracing paper
pencil
scrap paper
scissors
chinagraph pencil
opaque ceramic paints: white,
red and gold
fine artist's paintbrush
paint palette
cotton buds (swabs)

1 Clean the bottle. Trace the template at the back of the book, adjusting it to fit eight times around the bottle, then cut out the scallops.

4 Using the template design as a guide, paint a four-petalled flower in gold paint between each scallop in the first round. Then fill in the centres of the daisies in gold paint.

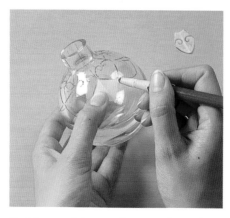

2 Use a chinagraph pencil to draw around scallop A eight times, fitting it close to the neck of the bottle. Draw in the curls, then draw around scallop B, fitting it between the first scallops.

5 Using the fine paintbrush, add tiny dots of white, gold and pink paint in delicate swags and lines to link the flowers. Fill in the gold ovals, and pink and white dots at the top of each heart, then complete the design with two small gold dots at the base of each pink daisy. Extend the design with rows of tiny dots up the neck of the perfume bottle.

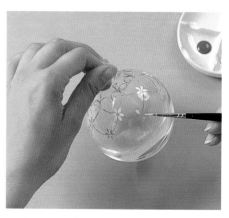

3 Using white, paint a six-petalled daisy at the base of each upper scallop. Mix a little red paint with white, and paint eight pink daisies at the base of each lower scallop.

6 Paint a large pink daisy exactly in the centre of the bottle stopper and add a gold centre to the daisy shape, as well as rows of tiny white dots radiating from the petals. Leave the paint to dry completely, then rub off the pencil marks using a cotton bud (swab). Bake the bottle and stopper to harden the paint, if necessary, following the manufacturer's instructions.

This cabinet uses opaque enamels rather than transparent glass paints, in the tradition of Eastern European folk art. Folk art relies on basic colour combinations and simple brushwork.

Folk Art Cabinet

You will need

small, glass-fronted display cabinet

reusable putty adhesive

fine artist's paintbrush

acrylic enamel paints: white, light green, deep green, red, raw sienna and yellow

paint palette

1 Enlarge the template from the back of the book and stick it to the back of the glass door with reusable putty adhesive. Paint the design on to the front of the glass using white acrylic enamel paint. Leave to dry.

2 Remove the template from the back of the glass. Paint over the leaves with the light green enamel paint, and leave to dry.

3 Paint a line of deep green paint along the lower edge of each of the light green leaves.

4 Paint the flowers with the red paint and then carefully blend in a little white towards the tips.

5 Paint over the stalk lines, half with raw sienna and half with yellow. Leave to dry.

Glass is a versatile medium to work with and can be used to create all sorts of decorative items from trinket boxes to lanterns. Using glass that you have painted, or ready-coloured glass panels, learn to cut it safely and accurately into intricate shapes. With pieces cut to size, you can solder them together to form three-dimensional functional pieces, or learn to add lead came to replicate stained-glass windows.

Working
with Glass

Glorious Glassware

There is a lot more to glass than a flat surface on which to paint patterns or pictures. As a material, it provides a wonderfully versatile basis for a variety of applications. Stained glass is the most obvious one, where pieces of coloured glass are fixed together with strips of lead to create glorious patterns and pictures. Stained glass need not be as ambitious as that seen in church and cathedral windows – simple shaped dec-

orations can be made to hang in a window, so the sunlight can sparkle through the glass, or on a Christmas tree where the tree lights can brighten the rich colours of the decoration. Jewel-bright glass nuggets can be used together with coloured glass pieces for a three-dimensional effect.

In addition to creating pictures and decorations for the window, coloured

glass can be used to make vases, pots, trinket boxes and simple lanterns. The more ambitious could even create entire leaded door panels. Although not for the novice, this type of glasswork is only a step on from creating pictures, hangings and plaques.

The traditional method of making stained glass involves cutting and soldering the individual pieces of glass together using copper foil and lead, but there is a far simpler and quicker way of creating a similar effect using self-adhesive lead strips. These are simply attached to the top of the glass to create the outlines of the design, and there is no cutting or soldering involved.

Glass cutting is not just for the professionals, and even the most experienced glass worker has to start somewhere. To minimize risks of cutting yourself on broken glass, always follow safety procedures, wear the correct clothing and protect your

eyes with goggles – no matter how small the task in hand. Similarly, soldering can appear to be quite a daunting task. Learning to use equipment and materials properly will remove the fear. As with most things, you will find that the more often you practise, the more proficient you will become, and the more you will enjoy the versatility of this skilled craft.

A variety of materials is needed for working with glass, which include glass paints, solder and flux, all of which are readily available from specialist glass shops.

Materials

lengths. The central bar or heart keeps two pieces of glass apart when put together. The flat strips at the top and bottom of the heart – the leaf – will stop the glass from falling out. Always wear rubber (latex) gloves or barrier cream when using lead.

Self-adhesive lead

This stick-on lead strip can be used to reproduce real lead came. Ensure a good seal by rubbing the lead with a boning peg, or the back of a teaspoon. Do not smoke or handle food while using lead, and keep it away from children. Wash your hands after use.

Solder

Made up of equal parts of tin and lead.

Tinned copper wire

This can be soldered easily. You can also tin wire with a soldering iron.

Ultraviolet glue

This glue hardens in daylight. It will not harden behind red glass, which blocks UV rays.

You will need the following items: acetate, carbon paper, clear varnish, contour paste, glass nuggets, glass paints, masking tape, paper towels, cotton buds (swabs), reusable putty adhesive, silver jewellery wire, white spirit (paint thinner), stained glass.

Copper foil and wire

A self-adhesive, heat-resistant tape, copper foil comes in various widths. Use it to bind glass edges prior to soldering. Copper wire is malleable and ideal for hooks and decoration. It is compatible with tin solder.

Epoxy glue

This strong glue hardens in minutes.

Float glass

Glaziers sell this clear polished glass.

Flux

This is brushed on to copper foil to clean it and lower the melting point of the solder so it flows more easily.

Horseshoe nails

Use to hold glass pieces in place as you work. Easy to remove, they reduce the risk of damage to glass and lead.

Lead came

Use lead came for creating stained glass windows. Available in 2m/2¼yd

For decorative glasswork, you will need a range of tools to equip you for the basic skills of glass cutting and soldering. The most important of these are described or listed below.

Equipment

Lead knife
A lead knife has a curved blade to help when cutting lead came.

Lead vice
A lead vice is useful for stretching pieces of lead came before cutting.

Letherkin tool
This is used to open up the leaf of the lead came after you have cut it.

Protective goggles
These are vital for eye protection when cutting glass.

Scythe stone
This removes the sharp edges from cut glass. Use on every piece.

Soldering iron
Use a 75-watt soldering iron. You will need a stand for the hot iron.

Boning peg
Use to smooth down the adhesive lead to ensure good contact with the glass.

Cutting oil
This oil lubricates the cutting wheel of a glass cutter and helps to prevent small particles of glass from binding to the wheel.

Fid
A fid is used for pressing down copper foil and self-adhesive lead.

Flux brush
These inexpensive brushes are used to paint flux on copper foil.

Glass cutter
Run the wheel of a glass cutter over the glass to be cut, to create a score mark. The glass will break on the line when stressed.

Grozing pliers
These are used to take off any sharp shards of glass.

Tallow stick
This is the traditional alternative to liquid soldering flux.

You will also find the following items useful: cotton rags, craft knife, jewellery pliers, nail polish remover, paintbrushes, pencils and pens, pliers, rubber (latex) gloves, ruler, scissors, self-healing cutting mat, sponges, thick straightedge, wire cutters, wire (steel) brush, wire (steel) wool.

Before you begin to tackle any of the projects in this chapter, look through this section, which acts as an introduction to the basic skills you will need for working with glass with assurance.

Techniques

Cutting glass   Measure accurately the area of glass you want to cut. There is no margin for error and mistakes cannot be rectified.

1 Hold the cutter so that your index finger is on top, your thumb and second finger grip each side, and the grozing teeth face towards your elbow. When you cut correctly with the cutter at a right angle to the glass, this position will give you movement in your arm.

2 Always cut the glass from edge to edge, one cut at a time. So start at one edge of the glass, with your cutter at right angles. Make one continuous cut from one edge to the other.

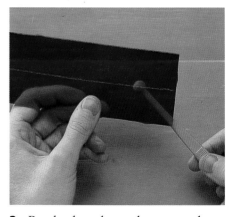

3 Break the glass where you have made the score mark. Hold the cutter upside down between your thumb and first finger. Hold it loosely so that you can swing it to hit the underside of the score mark with the ball on the end of the cutter. Tap along the score mark. The glass will break.

4 Alternatively, hold the glass at each side of the score mark. Apply firm pressure pulling down and away from the crack. Use this method for very straight lines.

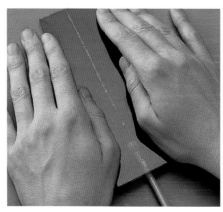

5 You could try putting the cutter on the table with the glass on the cutter and score mark over the cutter. With the base of your thumbs put pressure on both sides of the score mark.

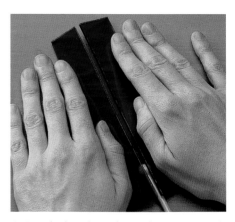

6 Break the glass along the score mark as shown. Smooth the edges and remove any sharp points with a scythe stone. Use a little water to lubricate the stone.

Foiling glass

Edging glass with copper foil allows you to solder pieces of glass together to create stained-glass effects. This technique is simple to do.

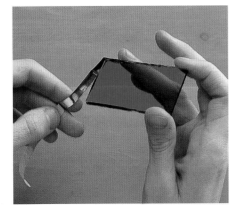

1 Hold the foil between your fingers, and use your thumb to peel back the protective backing paper as you work around the glass. Try not to touch the adhesive side of the tape – it will not stick if it is greasy or dusty.

2 Stick the foil to the edge of the piece of glass, working all the way around it, and overlapping the end of the foil by 1cm/½in.

3 Using two fingertips, press the foil down on to both sides of the glass, all the way around. Now use the fid to flatten the foil on to the glass to ensure it is stuck firmly all the way around.

Soldering glass

Soldering is the technique of joining pieces of metal together, in this case copper foil-edged glass. This is a technique that requires some practice to achieve a neat, professional finish.

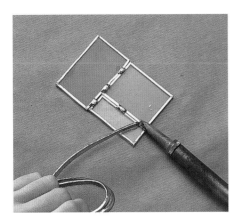

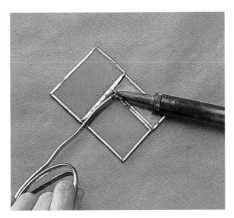

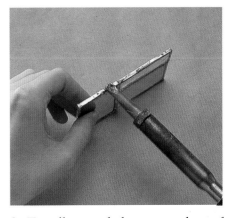

1 Using a flux brush, apply the flux to all the copper foil showing on the first side. Take the soldering iron so the tip of the iron side faces side to side and the thin side faces up and down. Hold the solder in the other hand with 10cm/4in uncoiled. Tack the pieces together by melting blobs of solder on to each joining edge. This holds the pieces while you solder them together.

2 Melt the solder, and allow it to run along the copper. Do not let it go too flat, but make sure you are always working with a small drop of solder. This makes it look neater and, even more importantly, is stronger. Turn the piece over and flux and solder the edges on the other side.

3 Tin all around the outer edges of the glass by firstly fluxing, and then running the soldering iron along the edges. There is usually enough solder from joining the inner edges to spread around the outside.

Using self-adhesive lead

Using self-adhesive lead is quick and easy. The skill is in the preparation: always ensure that the surface of the glass is scrupulously clean.

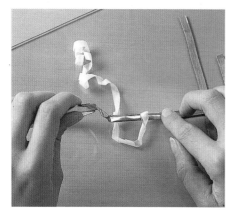

1 Clean the glass. Peel off the backing from the lead and press one end of it down gently with your fingers. Use one hand to hold the end while you bend the lead to fit the design. Always wash your hands after handling lead.

2 Trim the end with scissors. It is important that the lead strip is firmly stuck to the glass so that paint will not leak underneath it. After applying the strip, burnish it using a boning peg or the back of an old teaspoon.

Using lead came

This technique requires skill, but it is within everyone's reach. As special tools are needed for this technique, it can be expensive.

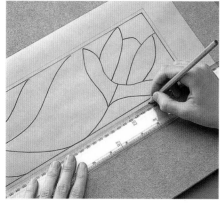

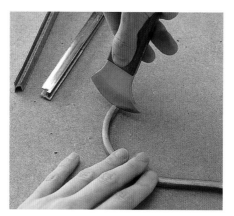

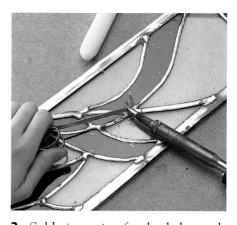

1 Draw the outline of each piece of glass that makes up the design. This outline represents the central point of the lead. Cut each piece of glass on the inside of the outline. To stretch the lead came to remove any kinks and make it easier to shape and cut, secure a spring-loaded vice to your bench and place one end of the came in it. Pull the other end with flat-nosed pliers. Do not break the lead.

2 Using a lead knife, bend the came to the shape of the edge of the glass. Using the knife blade, mark across the leaf where it will be cut (leave it a little short to accommodate the leaf of the piece crossing it). Place the came leaf on a flat surface. Position the knife and push down in a gentle but firm rocking motion until you are right through the came. Cut directly down and not at an angle.

3 Soldering wire for leaded panels contains lead, so wear barrier cream to protect your hands. Holding the soldering wire in your left hand, lower the tip of the soldering iron for a few seconds to melt the solder and join the separate pieces of lead came securely together.

This impressive panel is in the style of pictorial windows which were fashionable adornments for doors and porches in the 1930s. A gallant ship tossed on huge waves was a popular subject for this treatment.

Stained-glass Window

You will need

pane of glass to fit window

nail polish remover or glass cleaner

paper towels

scrap paper

felt-tipped pen

reusable putty adhesive

adhesive lead strip

tin snips or old scissors

boning peg or teaspoon

glass paints: red, yellow, dark blue, turquoise, white

medium and fine artist's paintbrushes

paint tray

1 Clean the glass to remove traces of grease. Draw a ship with hull and sails and waves on scrap paper to fit your panel and attach it to the underside of the glass using reusable putty adhesive.

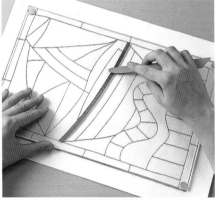

2 Peel the backing paper off a length of adhesive lead strip and place it over the line illustrating the hull of the boat. Trim the strip at the end with tin snips or old scissors, and smooth it down firmly using a boning peg or the back of a teaspoon, to ensure a good contact with the glass.

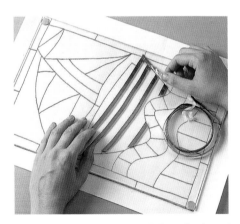

3 Repeat for the rest of the planks of the hull. Complete the outline of the boat, placing the strips over the ends of the previous ones. Trim the ends of the outline, and smooth down with either the boning peg or teaspoon.

4 Attach the lead strips for the waves, positioning the long strips first. Ease the strips around the curves with your fingers. Complete the boat mast, sails and frame in the same way. Burnish all the lines with the boning peg or spoon, carefully smoothing the fullness on the inside of the curves. ▶

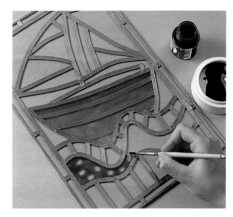

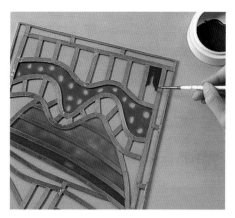

5 Mix burnt orange from the red and yellow paint and add a touch of dark blue. Paint the top plank of the hull with orange. For the next plank, mix a brighter orange. Add more of the yellow still to make light orange for the third plank, and paint the lowest plank yellow.

6 Fill in the central wave with the turquoise paint, leaving some small randomly spaced circles of clear glass.

7 Use dark blue to paint around the edge of the first panel in the lowest part of the sea. Mix the paint with white and add a pale blue strip down the middle of the panel while the dark blue is still wet. Draw the edges of the colours together for a marbled effect.

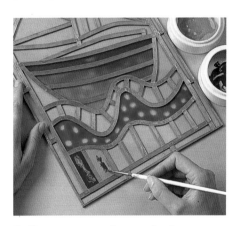

8 Repeat in each panel, alternating the colours. Above the wave, paint alternate panels dark or pale blue, leaving the remaining panels clear.

9 Mix the red with dark blue to make purple, and paint the cabin roof. Paint alternate panels of the sails yellow, then add a little blue paint to make a light green colour for the remaining parts of the sails.

10 Mix white with the light green and use to paint alternate panels of the frame. Paint the flag with the red paint. Mix turquoise with pale blue for the remaining panels of the frame. Leave the glass panel to dry completely.

Give your pictures a touch of grandeur with this richly coloured frame made from glass paints and stick-on lead in an abstract linear design. Choose colours to complement those in the picture you are framing.

Leaded Picture Frames

You will need
clean glass clip-frame
paper
pen and pencil
metal ruler
indelible black felt-tipped pen
3mm/⅛in self-adhesive lead
craft knife
self-healing cutting mat
boning peg
glass paints
paintbrush

1 Remove the clips and backing board from the clip-frame. Place the glass on a piece of paper and draw around it to create a template of the right dimensions.

2 Using a pencil and metal ruler, draw a simple linear design on the template. Place the glass over the template and trace the design on to the glass using an indelible black felt-tipped pen.

3 Stretch the lead by pulling it gently. Cut four lengths to fit around the outside edge of the frame, using a sharp craft knife and a cutting mat. Remove the backing paper from the lead and stick the lead in place.

4 Measure the lead needed for the inner framework and cut with a craft knife by using a side-to-side rocking motion. Hold the knife blade at a 90-degree angle to the lead to ensure a straight cut. Work on a cutting mat. With the edges butted closely together, peel away the backing paper from the lead strips and press gently into place with your fingertips.

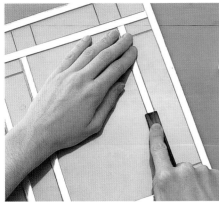

5 Once the lead is in the correct position, press firmly along its length using a boning peg to seal it to the glass.

6 With the pointed end of the boning peg, press around the outer edges of each strip of lead. This will tidy the edges and prevent the glass paints from seeping underneath the strips.

7 Colour in the design using glass paints. Leave to dry. Replace the backing board, add a picture of your choice and clip the frame into place.

This plain vase has been given a stained-glass effect with the use of vivid paints and patterns of stick-on lead. Filling the vase with water will ensure that the horizontal lines of the border will be accurate.

Banded Vase

You will need

clean, square vase
water-based felt-tipped pen
ruler
black contour paste
sponge scourer
scissors
glass paints: yellow, orange, red and violet
colourless medium
spatula
craft knife
self-healing cutting mat
3mm/⅛in self-adhesive lead
fid

1 Gauge by eye the position of the borders. Using a water-based felt-tipped pen, draw the position of the lower border. Pour water into the vase up to this point. Stand the vase on a level surface and draw around the vase at the water level.

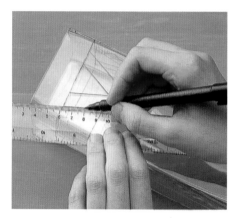

2 Mark the position of the top border. Top up the water to this level and draw the second line around the vase. Empty the vase. Mark the simple pattern on to the surface of the vase with the felt-tipped pen and a ruler.

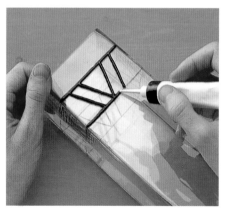

3 Go over the lines with the black contour paste and leave it to dry. Cut a sponge scourer into pieces to match the shapes of the design.

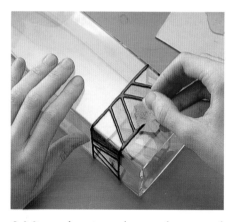

4 Mix each paint colour with an equal amount of colourless medium and sponge the paint over the vase using a different piece of sponge for each colour. Leave to dry for 24 hours.

5 Using a craft knife, score around the edge of each area of colour. Use the tip of the craft knife to lift up the contour paste and carefully peel it off the vase.

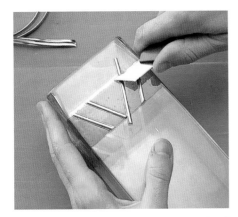

6 Cut pieces of self-adhesive lead slightly oversize for all of the shorter lines. Peel off the backing paper and press them in place. Trim the ends of each piece of lead at an angle with a craft knife.

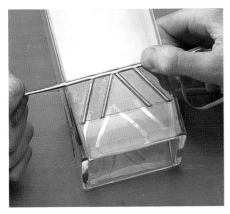

7 Cut two strips of lead for the two border lines and press them into place.

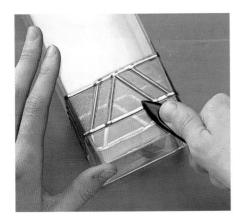

8 Rub over all the lead lines with a fid to press them firmly in place.

This piece of decorated glass creates beautiful shimmering patterns as it catches the light. The design is traced directly on to the glass with contour paste then coloured with glass paints.

Heart Light Catcher

You will need

paper

2mm/¹⁄₁₆in float glass

glass cutter

cutting oil

thick straightedge

self-adhesive copper foil tape

fid

1mm/¹⁄₂₅in tinned copper wire

wire cutters

round-nosed pliers

straight-nosed pliers

flux and flux brush

solder and soldering iron

black contour paste

glass paints: yellow, green, pink, blue and red

fine artist's paintbrush

paint palette

toothpick

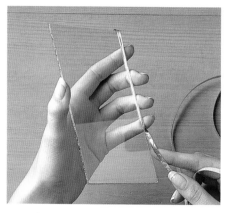

1 Enlarge the template from the back of the book and cut a piece of float glass to fit the design. Wash the glass and edge it with self-adhesive copper foil tape. Press down with a fid.

2 Bend the wire into two small circular hanging loops using round-nosed pliers. Grip the wire in the middle and bend the ends down to form an upside-down "U". With straight-nosed pliers, grip each arm of the "U" and bend up to form a 90-degree angle. Bend the arms downwards with round-nosed pliers.

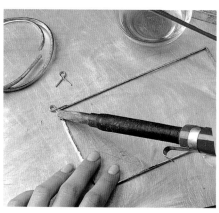

3 Brush the copper-foiled edge with flux, and then tin (see Window Hanging, step 4). Solder the hanging hoops in place. Wash the glass.

4 Lay the template on a work surface and place the light catcher over it. Trace the design on to the glass with black contour paste. Leave to dry.

5 Paint the glass, following the final photograph for the colours. Use the toothpick to decorate the design with scratchwork.

This vase evokes the work of the designer Charles Rennie Mackintosh. Self-adhesive lead is used to create the effect of leaded glasswork and is simply pressed on to the glass surface for a decorative effect.

Cherry Blossom Vase

You will need

paper

pencil

vase

reusable putty adhesive

self-adhesive lead, 3mm/⅛in and 4mm/³⁄₁₆in wide

scissors or craft knife

fid or wooden peg

glass paints: white and pink

matt varnish

paint-mixing palette

fine artist's paintbrush

1 Enlarge the template from the back of the book to fit your vase. Stick it to the inside of the vase with reusable putty adhesive. Using the template as a guide, bend and stick the pieces of 3mm/⅛in-wide self-adhesive lead down over all of the bold lines on the template. Use scissors or a strong craft knife to trim the ends.

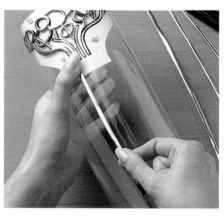

2 For the stem lines, cut two strips of 3mm/⅛in-wide self-adhesive lead the same length as your vase, and a further two 4mm/³⁄₁₆in-wide lead strips. Press the end of each into place to join the stems on the upper design and then run them down the length of the vase.

3 Splay the ends slightly at the base, and trim them so that they all end at the same point.

4 Cut a piece of 4mm/³⁄₁₆in-wide lead long enough to go around the vase with a little spare. Press it around the vase, just overlapping the edges of the stem lines. To smooth the joins, rub over with a fid or wooden peg.

5 Mix a little white paint with matt varnish. Do the same with a little pink paint. Apply the white paint sparingly to fill the blossom shapes, adding just a touch of pink to each area.

The etched glass panels on this old door have been painted with coloured glass paints and finished with stick-on lead strips. The finished effect has a lighter look than genuine stained glass.

Leaded Door Panels

You will need

door with two sandblasted
glass panels
tape measure
paper
pencil
ruler
black felt-tipped pen
scissors
masking tape
indelible black felt-tipped pen
self-adhesive lead, 1cm/⅜in wide
craft knife
self-healing cutting mat
boning peg
glass paints: turquoise, green, yellow
and light green
turpentine
fine artist's paintbrushes

1 Measure the glass panels with a tape measure. With a pencil, draw them to scale on a piece of paper. Using a ruler, draw your design within the panel area, including 1cm/⅜in wide dividing lines to allow for the leading. Trace over the design in felt-tipped pen, cross-hatching the lead lines.

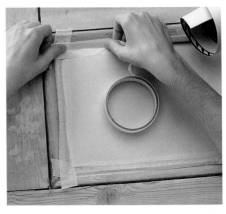

2 Cut out this paper pattern carefully with scissors and then stick it to the reverse of one of the glass panels by applying lengths of masking tape around the edges.

3 Trace the design from the pattern on to the sandblasted side of the glass with an indelible black felt-tipped pen. When the tracing is complete, remove the paper pattern.

4 Stretch the lead by gently pulling it. Cut four lengths to fit around the edge of the glass panel, using a sharp craft knife. Remove the backing paper and stick the lead in place.

5 Measure the lead needed for the inner framework and cut with a craft knife using a side-to-side rocking motion. Keep the blade at a 90° angle to the lead to ensure a straight cut. Cut and stick longer lengths of lead first, then work the smaller pieces.

6 With the edges butted closely together, remove the backing paper from the lead and press into place with your fingertips. Then press firmly along the length of the lead with a boning peg to seal it to the glass. Press around the outer edges of the lead lines with the pointed end of the boning peg in order to create a neat, watertight finish.

7 Dilute the glass paints with 30 per cent turpentine to create a subtle, watercolour feel to the paint. Use a small paintbrush to colour in the small areas between the leading. Clean the brushes with turpentine between the different colours.

8 Once the intricate areas are coloured in, paint the remainder of the design, leaving the centre of the glass panel unpainted. Alternatively, you could paint the whole area if you prefer. Repeat for the other panel.

The fresh white and green opal glass of this planter neatly hides the flowerpot inside, while the contrasting colours of the opal glass will complement the colour of the foliage.

Opal Glass Planter

You will need

tracing paper

black pen and paper

white and green opal glass

glass cutter

straightedge

round-nosed pliers

carbon paper

ballpoint pen

scythe stone

5mm/¼in-wide copper foil

fid

solder and soldering iron

flux

flux brush

washing-up liquid (dishwashing detergent)

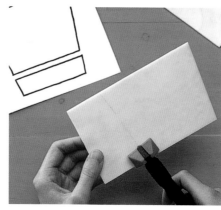

1 Trace the template from the back of the book, enlarging to the size required. Place the white glass over the template and score five identical pieces for the sides with a glass cutter, using a straightedge to ensure straight lines. Use a pair of round-nosed pliers to break the glass along the scorelines. Cut strips of green opal glass for the bottom of each panel.

2 Place carbon paper over the green glass, then put the template on top. Transfer the shape for the top sections with a pen. Score the straight lines using a straightedge as a guide. Score the curved edges and break them by tapping under the glass with the ball on the end of the glass cutter. Transfer and cut out the base design. Remove sharp edges with a scythe stone.

3 Wrap copper foil around the edge of each piece and use a fid to press the foil into place. Allow the soldering iron to heat up. Brush on flux and tack-solder together the three sections that make up each side panel.

4 Lightly tack-solder one of the side panels to the base, using a minimum of solder. Position the next panel and repeat. Tack the two panels together. Continue until all the pieces are in place on the base.

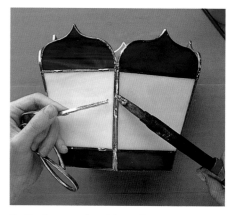

5 Reflux and solder all of the joints. Wash the planter thoroughly before use, with hot water and washing-up liquid (dishwashing detergent).

In this unusual project, different-sized glass nuggets are gradually built up one on top of another to create a colourful wall around the mirrored base of the bottle holder. Choose a whole rainbow of beautiful colours.

Glass Nugget Bottle Holder

You will need

self-healing cutting mat

pair of compasses (compass)

indelible black felt-tipped pen

mirror glass

bottle

glass cutter

square-nosed pliers

copper foil, 12mm/½in and 4mm/³⁄₁₆in wide

fid

solder

soldering iron

flux

flux brush

glass nuggets

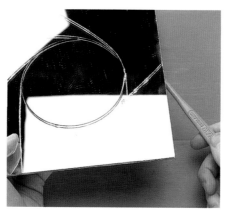

1 On a cutting mat draw a circle on mirror glass 2.5–4cm/1–1½in larger than the base of the bottle.

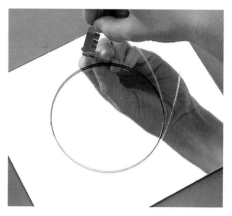

2 Score around the circle with a glass cutter. Draw lines from the edge of the circle to the edge of the mirror.

3 Tap on the reverse of the mirror with the ball of the glass cutter.

4 Loosen and then break off the excess mirror with square-nosed pliers.

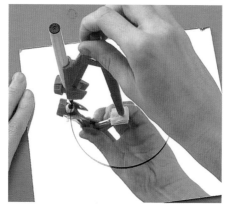

5 Wrap the 12mm/½in copper foil around the edge of the glass circle.

6 Press down with a fid and solder using flux and the soldering iron.

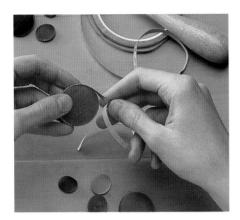

7 Select some of the coloured glass nuggets and wrap each one with the 4mm/³⁄₁₆in copper foil.

8 Solder the nuggets and start to build up an edge around the glass circle.

9 When the border is the required height, tidy up the inside and outside with the soldering iron to smooth out any drips of solder.

Slip this glass lantern over a night-light to create a colourful glow in the evenings. The lantern is made with two plain and two panelled sections of coloured glass.

Indoor Glass Lantern

You will need
tracing paper
pencil
ruler and pen (optional)
glass cutter
sheets of clear glass
sheets of stained glass: red,
orange and yellow
etching paste
medium artist's paintbrush
clean cotton rag
5mm/¼in copper foil
fid
flux and flux brush
solder and soldering iron
small box or block of wood
night-light
tile

1 Trace the templates for the indoor lantern from the back of the book. Enlarge to the size required using a ruler and pen or a photocopier.

2 Take a glass cutter and, using your templates as a guide, cut out two clear glass sides and the pieces of coloured glass for the other two sides. You will have four red pieces, three orange and three yellow.

4 Take the acid-etched glass to your sink and allow cold water to run freely over the glass to take the paste off. Rinse thoroughly and then dry with a clean cotton rag.

5 Wrap copper foil around the edges of all of the pieces of coloured and clear/etched glass. Using a fid, flatten all the copper foil to smooth around the edges.

3 Using the template as a guide, take each side and paint etching paste on in squares as shown. Leave the paste for 3 minutes.

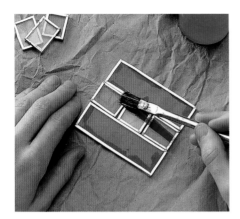

6 Place the pieces next to each other as you wish to solder them, panel by panel. Flux all the copper using a flux brush.

7 Tack each side together by melting a spot of solder on each joining edge. This keeps the pieces in place, and makes soldering easier.

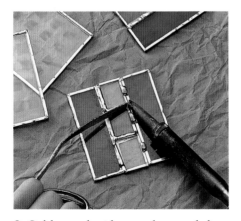

8 Solder each side together, and then solder around the edges to complete the four panels.

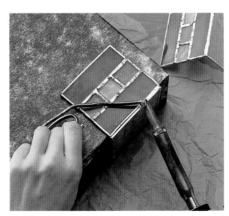

9 To solder the lantern together and make it three-dimensional you will need to balance the sides at a right angle on a small box or a block of wood. Flux and solder two corners so they can stand upright.

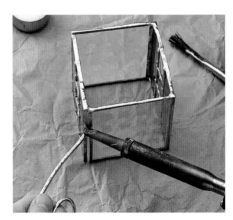

10 Solder the last two corners by fluxing and then soldering from top to bottom. Clean the glass with a clean cotton rag. Stand the night-light on a tile and place the lantern over it.

This plaque is made from pieces of stained glass and glass nuggets. Nuggets come in a wide range of colours and can add bright spots of colour among the crazy patchwork of glass.

Door Number Plaque

You will need

circle cutter

cutting oil

30cm/12in square of 3mm/⅛in

clear glass

piece of carpet or blanket

glass cutter

tracing paper

pencil

paper

indelible black felt-tipped pen

pieces of stained glass

scythe stone

glass nuggets

ultraviolet glue

lead came

lead knife

bradawl or drill

2mm/¹⁄₁₆in copper wire

round-nosed pliers

flux and flux brush

solder

soldering iron

black acrylic paint

tiling grout

grout spreader

clean cotton rag

Tip
Glass glue sets when it is exposed to ultraviolet light or sunlight.

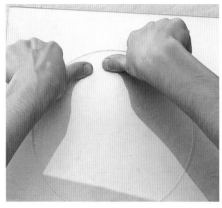

1 Set a circle cutter to cut a 20cm/8in diameter circle. Dip the cutter in oil, centre it in the glass square and score the circle in one sweep. Turn the glass over and place it on a piece of carpet or blanket on a work surface. Press down with both thumbs just inside the scoreline until the line begins to break. Repeat until the scoreline is broken all the way around.

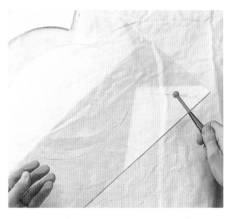

2 Use a glass cutter to score a line in from each corner of the glass square, stopping just before you reach the circle. With the ball of the glass cutter, tap behind each scored line until the glass cracks up to the circle. The side sections will fall away, releasing the circle.

3 Trace the required numbers from the back of the book, enlarging them to the size required. Draw around the circle of glass on to plain paper and write your own door number centrally using the template as a guide.

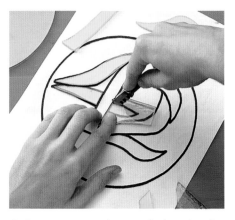

4 Score pieces of stained glass for the numerals. Break the glass by tapping behind the scoreline with the ball of the glass cutter. Remove any rough edges with a scythe stone. Centre the glass circle over the template.

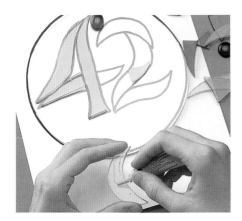

5 Arrange the numerals on the glass circle and place glass nuggets around them. Cut pieces of glass in contrasting colours to fill the spaces. Working away from sunlight, apply ultraviolet glue to the back of each piece and press it into place. When all of the pieces are glued, check the position of each and slide them into place.

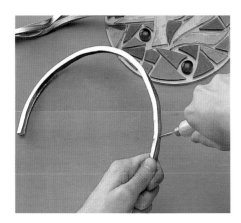

6 Use a lead knife to cut a length of lead came approximately 70cm/28in long. Use a bradawl or drill to make a small hole in the centre of the strip of came.

7 Cut a 10cm/4in length of copper wire. With a pair of round-nosed pliers, bend a hanging loop. Thread the ends through the hole in the came and bend them up to lock the loop in place. Wrap the came around the glass with the hanging loop at the top.

8 Trim off any excess lead came with the lead knife. Flux the joint and then lightly solder the ends together.

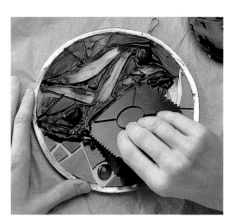

9 Mix some black paint with grout. Spread it over the surface, into the spaces between the glass. Remove any excess with a rag. Leave to dry, then polish with a clean cotton rag.

The type of paintwork used in this unusual window decoration is not very easy to control, and it is precisely this free-flowing quality that gives the style its appeal.

Window Hanging

You will need

paper and pencil

glass, 3mm/⅛in thick

glass cutter

cutting oil

scythe stone

5mm/¼in self-adhesive copper foil tape

fid

red glass nuggets

flux and flux brush

solder and soldering iron

1mm/¹⁄₂₅in tinned copper wire

round-nosed pliers

straight-nosed pliers

black contour paste

paint-mixing palette

glass paints: blue, turquoise, red, yellow, violet and white

clear varnish

fine artist's paintbrush

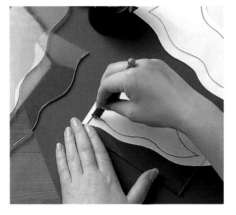

1 Enlarge the template at the back of the book to a size that is suitable for the window you wish to hang the pieces in. Lay a sheet of glass on the template and cut out five sections. (Have a glazier do this if you are not confident in cutting glass.)

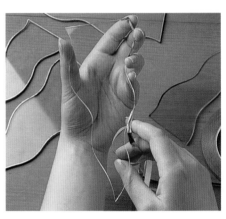

2 Wash all of the pieces to remove any traces of cutting oil. Remove any sharp edges with a scythe stone, then press self-adhesive copper foil tape over all of the edges. Press the foil down with a fid.

3 Using a scythe stone, lightly abrade the edge of each glass nugget. Wrap each nugget in copper foil tape.

4 Brush all of the copper-foiled edges with flux. Melt a bead of solder on to your soldering iron, and run the bead along the edge of each piece of glass to "tin" it with a thin coating of solder. Repeat as necessary until all of the edges are equally coated. Cut ten pieces of tinned copper wire 5cm/2in long for the hanging loops.

5 With round-nosed pliers, bend the ends down to form an upside-down "U". With straight-nosed pliers, grip each arm of the "U" and bend it up to form a 90-degree angle. Grip with round-nosed pliers while you bend the two arms downwards. Touch-solder the loops on the top of the glass pieces. Wash the pieces.

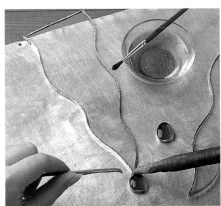

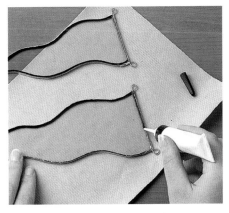

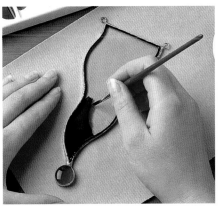

6 Apply flux to the end of one of the sections and one of the nuggets. Melt a bead of solder on to the iron and then solder the nugget in place. Melt on some more solder to ensure the nugget is secure.

7 Apply a line of black contour paste around the edge of each of the glass pieces in order to contain glass paint solution.

8 In a mixing palette, prepare the colours you wish to use. Mix each with equal parts of clear varnish and opaque white paint. Apply the colours thickly and freely, allowing them to blend into each other. Leave to dry for at least 24 hours.

These square and triangular stained-glass pendants are decorated with motifs cut from acetate. Hang them in a line on a gauzy fabric curtain to allow the sunlight and colours to really shine through.

Curtain Decorations

You will need

copyright-free pictures of shells

acetate

small, sharp scissors

pencil

paper

tracing paper

pieces of stained glass

glass cutter

4mm/³/₁₆in copper foil

fid

flux and flux brush

solder and soldering iron

epoxy glue

copper wire

small pliers

hooks and eyes

white sewing thread

sewing needle

white muslin (cheesecloth) curtain

curtain pole

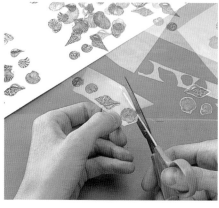

1 Photocopy pictures of shells on to acetate and cut them out with small, sharp scissors.

2 Trace the triangles and squares from the back of the book. Cut out glass shapes, using the templates as a guide.

3 Wrap copper foil around the edges of the larger pieces of glass.

4 Use a fid to flatten the edges of the copper foil around the pieces of glass.

◀ **5** Flux and solder the copper foil to make it silver. The heat will make the foil turn a silver colour.

▶ **6** Take a soldered piece of glass and a smaller piece of the same shape. Glue the pieces together, trapping the photocopy between the glass.

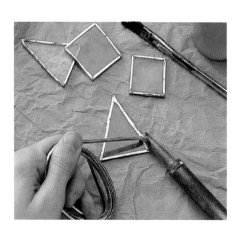

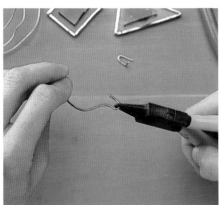

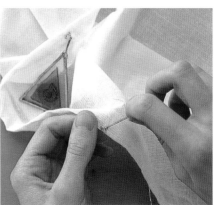

7 Using a pair of small pliers, bend the copper wire into small hooks. Make a separate hook for each decoration you have made.

8 Solder the hook to the copper foil around the edges of the decorations, remembering to flux the wire and the soldered edges.

9 Sew the eyes from several hooks and eyes to the top of the curtain and hook on the curtain decorations. Fold the curtain over a pole so the decorations are hanging in the top third of the window, as shown.

Opal glass is available from stained-glass specialists and has an extra special lustre. As this project involves cutting and soldering lots of small pieces, it is intended for the more experienced glassworker.

Trinket Box

You will need

carbon paper

paper

pencil

clear 2mm/¹⁄₁₆in picture glass

blue opal glass

mirrored blue stained glass

cutting square or straightedge

glass cutter

cutting oil

copper foil, 4mm/³⁄₁₆in and 5mm/¹⁄₄in

fid

flux

flux brush

soldering iron

solder

tinned copper wire

wire cutters

indelible black felt-tipped pen

scythe stone

round-nosed pliers

1 Enlarge the template from the back of the book to the size required. Transfer the shapes to the glass using carbon paper. Transfer the side pieces of the box on to clear glass and blue opal glass, and the octagonal base outline on to the mirrored blue glass. Score and break the glass using a thick straightedge or a cutting square.

2 Wrap the edges of the blue opal side pieces in 5mm/¹⁄₄in-wide copper foil and the edges of the thinner clear picture glass in the 4mm/³⁄₁₆in-wide copper foil. Press the foil down firmly using a fid.

3 Apply lines of 4mm/³⁄₁₆in-wide copper foil along the edges of the top surface of the mirror base to ensure that the sides bond firmly to the base. Wrap the sides in 5mm/¹⁄₄in-wide copper foil. Press down firmly with a fid.

4 Brush all of the copper-wrapped pieces with safety flux and lightly tack-solder the pieces into place, adjusting them slightly if necessary.

▶

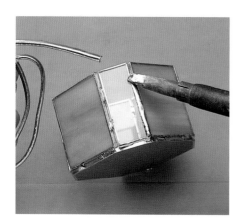

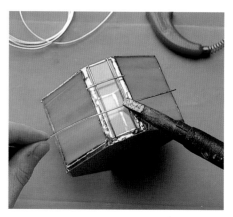

5 Reflux and solder all the copper surfaces. To give the edges a neat finish, run a bead of solder to fill the point where the side sections meet. Wash the box thoroughly to remove any traces of flux.

6 With the box balanced on one side, hold the end of a piece of wire just overlapping one of the clear sections. Brush with flux and touch the tip of the iron to the wire to solder it. Trim off the other end with wire cutters and repeat, using two vertical wires for each clear glass panel.

7 Solder two horizontal pieces of wire to each pair of verticals. Solder them on oversize, then trim them to length when they are soldered in place. Wash thoroughly to remove any traces of flux. Repeat steps 6 and 7 for each clear glass pane.

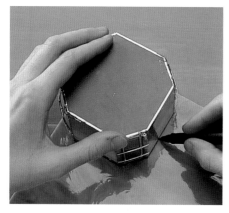

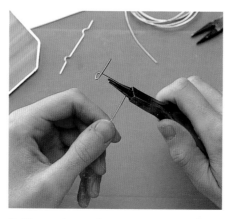

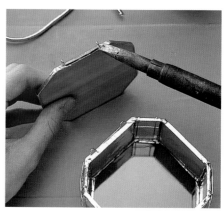

8 Choose some glass for the lid and place it with the side you want to be uppermost facing down. Place the box upside down over the glass and trace around the box with an indelible black felt-tipped pen. Score and break the glass just inside the lines. Remove any extra sharp edges with a scythe stone lubricated with a little water, then wrap the edges of the lid in 5mm/¼in-wide foil. Apply flux and plate the foil with solder.

9 Cut a piece of wire measuring about 10cm/4in long. Bend two kinks in the wire with a pair of round-nosed pliers, using the picture as a guide. Cut another 10cm/4in length of wire and bend two right angles in it to coincide with the kinks in the first wire. Bend the two ends into loops and trim off the excess wire with the wire cutters.

10 Apply flux to both pieces of wire. Solder the kinked length of wire to one side of the box and the looped piece to the lid. Wash both the box and the lid thoroughly to remove any traces of flux. Slot the lid hinge section into the body section to complete the trinket box.

This stained-glass project uses many glass pieces that are cut to shape to create an abstract design, ideal for the panel of a bathroom cabinet. It is an ambitious project.

Bathroom Cabinet Door Panel

You will need

tracing paper

pencil

ruler

felt-tipped pen

sheets of coloured glass

glass cutter

grozing pliers

masking tape

wooden board

three battens

hammer and horseshoe nails

lead knife

15mm/⅝in lead came

letherkin tool

barrier cream

wire (steel) brush

tallow

clean cotton rags

solder wire and soldering iron

rubber (latex) gloves (optional)

black lead lighting putty

whiting powder

hard scrubbing brush

fire grate blackener

1 Trace the template from the back of the book, enlarging to the size required. The outer line represents the outer edge of the lead came. Go over the inner lines in felt-tipped pen. These thick lines will represent the centre of the pieces of lead came that join the glass together.

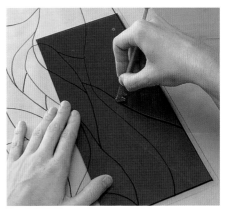

2 To cut out the coloured glass for the panel, lay a sheet of glass over the design and, starting from one corner, score along a line using a glass cutter. Carefully score along the other lines of the piece.

3 Use the ball end of the glass cutter to gently tap the reverse of the glass below the line you have scored. Tap until the two pieces fall apart. Use grozing pliers to nip off any small pieces of glass.

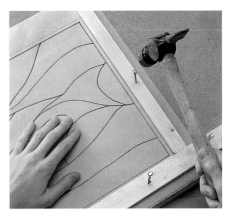

4 When all the glass is cut, tape your drawing to a wooden board. Nail one batten to each side edge and another to the bottom edge, along the outer pencil line of the rectangle.

▶

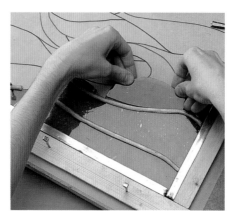

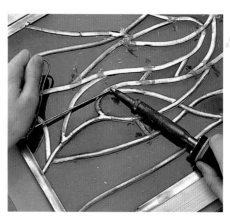

5 Using a lead knife, mark and cut a piece of lead came to fit along the side of the panel. Repeat for the bottom edge. Using a letherkin tool, open up the leaves of the lead to make it easier to insert the glass. Wear barrier cream to protect your hands from the toxic lead.

6 Build up the stained-glass design one piece at a time, cutting the lead came and inserting the glass carefully between the leaves of lead. Hammer horseshoe nails into the wooden board, as shown, to tack and hold the lead in place as you work.

7 When the design is finished, clean the lead joints with a wire (steel) brush. Rub tallow on to each joint. Place solder wire over the joint then melt into place with the soldering iron. When the front is finished, turn the panel over and repeat the process on the reverse.

8 Wearing barrier cream, use your thumbs to press black lead lighting putty firmly into the gaps between the lead came and the pieces of glass. Work around the border and all around the individual pieces.

9 Cover the glass panel liberally with whiting powder. This will absorb the excess oil in the putty and help it to dry more quickly. Leave to harden for 1–2 hours. Use a hard scrubbing brush to clean off the whiting and excess putty. Repeat steps 8 and 9 on the reverse of the panel.

10 Wearing barrier cream, coat the lead with fire grate blackener using a clean cotton rag, then polish off the excess until you get a deep colour.

Glass Mosaic

Mosaic is a craft achievable by complete beginners. Essentially, it is painting-by-numbers but with pieces of glass, known as tesserae, instead of paint. The skill lies in combining colours together in a pleasing way, and in producing a representative pictorial image. To start with, draw simple stylized shapes freehand or mark out geometric patterns on a plywood base, then fill in the designs with coloured glass tesserae.

Mosaic Masterpieces

Creating a glass mosaic is very satisfying, particularly for those who enjoy finely detailed work. Made with pieces of vitreous glass, a mosaic has a striking, fragmented look and a lovely textural finish. Vitreous glass tesserae are manufactured glass squares that can easily be cut into different shapes with tile nippers to fit a design. When embarking on your first mosaic, choose a small-scale, simple design to work on: an object such as a plant pot or house number plate is ideal. Geometric shapes, stripes and swirls work well. Often, these simple designs can produce the

most effective mosaics. Concentrate on combining different colours in the tesserae you choose. Lay the tesserae side-by-side and look at the effect of the different elements. When the combinations work, you can commit yourself to sticking the tesserae to the base.

Mosaics can be flat and two-dimensional, such as plaques, panels and picture frames, or they can be three-dimensional, such as those decorating trinket boxes, bottles and plant pots. With two-

dimensional mosaic it is possible to see how the colours work together in an instant, unlike three-dimensional designs. Dark and light tesserae placed side-by-side produce a bold, striking effect while colours with similar tonal value produce a more subtle shading.

In a mosaic, grout can be as important as the tesserae. It holds the pieces together and unifies the design. Grout is available in powder form or ready mixed in white, beige, grey and black. It is

possible to add acrylic paint or dye to the grout mix in a colour that is appropriate for your colour scheme to offset the mosaic. Determine what role the

grout should play, and therefore what colour it should be, when planning your design.

In this chapter, you will find plenty of ideas for making door plaques, mosaic lanterns, plant pots, boxes, bottles, tables and even a stained-glass screen. Follow the projects step-by-step, or use them as a springboard for your own creative ideas for mosaics.

The main materials used in mosaic are the individual pieces, known as tesserae, which can be ceramic, glass, china or any solid material. The other important materials are the grout and the rigid base.

Materials

Adhesives
There are several ways of attaching tesserae to a background. Cement-based tile adhesive is the most well known, and it can also be used to grout between the tesserae once the design is complete. For a wood base, use PVA (white) glue. For a glass base, use a silicone-based or a clear, all-purpose adhesive. To stick glass to metal, use epoxy resin. PVA is also used to prime a wooden base to make a suitable surface for the mosaic.

Admix
This is added to tile adhesive for extra adhesion.

Bases
Mosaic can be made on top of almost any rigid and pre-treated surface. One of the most popular bases is plywood.

Brown paper
This is used as backing for mosaics created by the semi-indirect method. Use the heaviest available.

Grout
Specialist grouts are smoother than tile adhesive and are available in a variety of colours.

Shellac
Use this to seal finished mosaics, especially those for outside use.

Tesserae
Mosaic pieces are described as tesserae.

Ceramic tiles – These are available in a range of colours and textures, glazed or unglazed. Household tiles can be cut to size using a hammer, or tile nippers for precise shapes.

China – Old china makes unusual tesserae. It creates an uneven surface, so is suitable for decorative projects rather than flat, functional surfaces. Break up china using a hammer.

Marble – Marble can be bought pre-cut into small squares; to cut it with accuracy you need specialist tools.

Mirror glass – Shards of mirror add a reflective sparkle to a mosaic. Mirror can be cut with tile nippers or glass cutters, or broken with a hammer.

Smalti – This is opaque glass that has been cut into regular chunks. It has a softly reflective surface.

Vitreous glass tesserae – These are glass squares which are corrugated on the back to accommodate tile adhesive. They are hardwearing and thus perfect for outdoor projects.

Many of the tools needed to make mosaics are ordinary household equipment; the rest can be purchased in a good hardware store. A pair of tile nippers is the main piece of specialist equipment you will need.

Equipment

Protective goggles
Wear safety goggles when you cut or smash tiles, and when working with hydrochloric acid.

Sacking (heavy cloth)
Use to wrap up tiles before breaking them with a hammer.

Sandpaper
Use coarse-grade sandpaper to prepare wood. To clean finished mosaics, use fine-grade sandpaper and wear a mask.

Saw
Use to cut wooden base material. Use a hacksaw for basic shapes, and a jigsaw for more complicated designs.

Spatula/Spreader/Squeegee
Used for spreading glue or other smooth adhesives, such as cellulose filler, on to your base material.

Clamps or bench vice
These are needed when cutting out the wooden base for projects.

Dilute hydrochloric acid
Use to clean cement-based grout from the finished mosaic if necessary. Always wear protective clothing, and work in a well-ventilated area.

Drill
A hand electric drill is needed for hanging projects on the wall.

Glass cutter
Use to cut or score glass tesserae.

Paint scraper
This is used to remove awkward pieces of dried tile adhesive or grout from the surface of a completed mosaic.

Protective face mask
You are strongly advised to wear a dust mask when you are mixing powdered grout, sanding the finished mosaic, and cleaning with hydrochloric acid.

Tile nippers
These are invaluable for cutting shaped tiles, especially curves.

You will also find the following items useful: bradawl, chalk, craft knife, flexible knife, rubber (latex) gloves, hammer, felt-tipped pen, masking tape, mixing container, nailbrush, paintbrushes, pencil, plastic spray bottle, pliers, ruler, scissors, set square, sponge, tape measure.

Read the instructions below carefully before beginning a mosaic project and choose the methods most appropriate to the design that you are creating. Remember to wear protective clothing.

Techniques

Cutting tesserae

There are two methods of cutting tesserae, one using tile nippers and one using a hammer. Choose the method depending on the shape of tesserae you require.

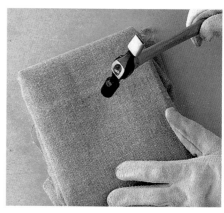

1 Using tile nippers and wearing goggles, hold a tessera between the tips of the nippers, and squeeze the handles together. It should break along the line of impact. To cut a specific shape, nibble at the edges.

2 Use a hammer to break up larger pieces such as household tiles and china, where regular shapes are not required. Remember to wear protective goggles.

3 When working with a hammer it is also advisable to wrap each tile or plate in a piece of sacking or heavy cloth to prevent flying shards.

Cutting glass

This technique requires practice and is potentially more dangerous. Wear protective goggles and follow the instructions below.

2 Applying firm, even pressure, score a line across in a single movement, without a break. You can either push the cutter away from you or pull it towards you. Don't score over the same line; if you make a mistake, try again on another part of the glass.

3 Hold the scored piece of glass in one hand. With your working hand, place pliers along the scored line and grip them firmly.

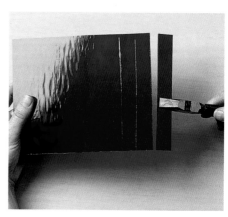

1 Holding the glass cutter, rest your index finger along the top. Hold the cutter at a 90-degree angle to the glass.

4 Angle the tip of the pliers up and pull down. The glass should break cleanly in two along the scored line.

Direct method

This is a popular technique, in which the tesserae are stuck, face up, on to the base and grouted into place. On a three-dimensional object or uneven surface this may be the only suitable method.

1 Cover the base with adhesive. Press the tesserae into it, cover with grout, leave to dry, then clean.

2 If you are following a design drawn on the base as a guide, apply a thin layer of tile adhesive on to the wrong side of each individual tessera and stick it into place.

3 If the tesserae are reflective, such as mirror glass or gold or silver smalti, try placing them at slightly different angles on a three-dimensional surface, to catch the light.

Semi-indirect method

With this method the tesserae are glued to the design off-site, but are then set into the tile adhesive in the final position.

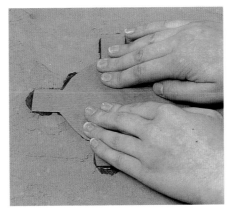

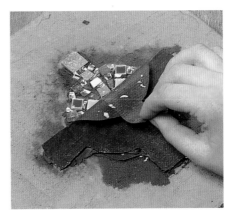

1 Draw a design on to brown paper. Adhere the tesserae right side down on to the paper using PVA (white) glue and a brush or palette knife.

2 Spread tile adhesive over the area designated for the mosaic. Press the mosaic into the adhesive, paper side up. Leave to dry for at least 24 hours.

3 Dampen the paper with a wet sponge and peel it off. The mosaic is now ready to be grouted and cleaned.

Indirect method
This technique originated as a way of making large mosaics off-site so that they could be transported ready-made. The design is divided into manageable sections which are fitted together on-site.

1 Make a wooden frame to the size required, securing the corners with 2.5cm/1in screws. Make a brown paper template of the inside of the frame. Draw a design on the design area of the paper, leaving a 5mm/¼in margin all around. Grease the inside of the frame with petroleum jelly.

2 Wearing protective goggles and gloves, cut the tesserae as required. Glue them right side down on the brown paper, using water-soluble adhesive and following the design. Leave to dry.

3 Place the wooden frame carefully over the mosaic, then sprinkle dry sand over the mosaic, using a soft brush to spread it into the crevices between the tesserae.

4 Wearing a face mask, on a surface that cannot be damaged, mix 3 parts sand with 1 part cement. Make a well in the centre, add water and mix it with a trowel until you have a firm consistency. Gradually add more water, if necessary, until the mortar is pliable but not runny.

5 Half-fill the frame with mortar, pressing it into the corners. Cut a square of chicken wire a little smaller than the frame. Place it on top of the mortar so that the wire does not touch the frame. Fill the rest of the frame with mortar, then smooth the surface. Cover with damp newspaper, then heavy plastic sheeting, and leave to dry thoroughly for 5–6 days.

6 Turn the frame over. Dampen the brown paper with a wet sponge and then carefully peel it off. Loosen the screws and remove the frame from the mosaic. The mosaic is now ready to be grouted and cleaned.

Grouting

Mosaics are grouted to give them extra strength and a smoother finish. Grout binds the tesserae together. Coloured grout is often used to unify the design; this can either be purchased as ready-made powder, or you can add dye or acrylic paint to plain grout.

1 When grouting three-dimensional objects or uneven surfaces, it is easiest to spread the grout with a flexible knife or spreader.

2 Rub the grout deep into the crevices in between the tesserae. Always wear rubber (latex) gloves when you are handling grout directly.

3 To grout large, flat mosaics, you can use powdered tile adhesive. Spoon it on to the surface, then spread it with a soft brush to fill all the crevices between the tesserae.

4 When you have completed the grouting process, spray the adhesive with water from a plastic spray bottle. You may need to repeat the process to achieve a smooth finish.

Cleaning

It is advisable to get rid of most of the excess grout while it is still wet. Most purpose-made grouts can be scrubbed from the surface using a stiff-bristled nailbrush and then polished off.

Cement mortars and cement-based adhesives need rougher treatment, and you will probably need to use sandpaper. A fast alternative is to dilute hydrochloric acid and then paint it on to the surface to dissolve the excess cement. The process should be done outside, as it gives off toxic fumes. When the excess cement has fizzed away, wash off the residue of acid from the mosaic with plenty of water. Remember to wear a face mask when sanding, and a face mask, goggles and gloves when using hydrochloric acid.

A mosaic door plaque adds a distinctive touch to your home and will withstand all weathers. Plan the design carefully so that you have space between the numbers and the border to fit neatly cut tesserae.

Door Number Plaque

You will need

scissors

craft paper

floor tile

pencil

metal ruler

vitreous glass tesserae: turquoise, black and yellow

PVA (white) glue

glue brush

tile nippers

cement-based powdered grout

notched spreader

sponge

cement-based tile adhesive

lint-free cloth

1 Cut a piece of craft paper the same size as the tile. Mark the border and number in reverse on the shiny side of the paper. The border is one tessera wide. There should be room between the border and numbers to insert a quarter-tessera neatly.

2 Dilute the PVA (white) glue to a 50/50 solution with water. Glue the flat sides of the turquoise tesserae on to the border of the craft paper, with a single black tessera at each corner of the plaque.

3 Cut some black tesserae with the tile nippers to make rectangles. Glue the black rectangles flat-side down over the paper numbers.

4 Cut the yellow tesserae into quarter-squares. Lay them around the straight edges of the numbers, using the tile nippers to cut to size as necessary. Glue them flat-side down as before. Place quarter-square yellow tesserae all around the curved edges of the numbers, cutting as necessary.

5 Mix the grout according to the manufacturer's instructions. Grout the mosaic with the spreader, removing the excess with a damp sponge. Leave to dry. Spread a layer of tile adhesive over the floor tile and key (scuff) with the notched edge of the spreader.

6 Place the grouted mosaic paper-side down on a flat surface. Place the floor tile on top, matching corners and edges. Press the tile down, wipe away excess adhesive and leave to dry.

7 Using a sponge and water, soak the paper on the front of the mosaic. Leave for 15 minutes.

8 Lift one corner of the paper to see if it comes away cleanly. If it does, peel the paper off carefully. If it proves difficult, leave it to soak a little longer and then try lifting it again.

9 Wipe away any surplus glue. Re-grout the plaque, including the sides. Remove excess grout with a damp sponge, then polish the surface with a dry, lint-free cloth.

This lantern is made by using a plain drinking glass as the base for a mosaic of tiny stained-glass squares, applied around the outside – a good way to use up glasses you're not too fond of.

Mosaic Lantern

You will need

indelible black felt-tipped pen

metal straightedge

pieces of stained glass: blue, green, red and yellow

glass cutter

ultraviolet glue

heavy-based glass tumbler

spatula and bowl

tile grout

black acrylic paint

sponge scourer

night-light

1 Using an indelible black felt-tipped pen and a metal straightedge, mark a neat grid of squares on each of the different coloured pieces of stained glass. Each square needs to measure 1cm/⅜in.

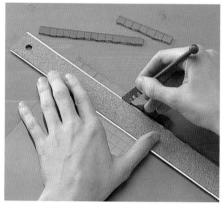

2 Cut the glass into 1cm/⅜in-lengths by scoring the glass with a glass cutter, using the straightedge as a guide. Tap underneath the score line with the ball end of the glass cutter, and then snap the glass apart gently between both thumbs.

3 Score the glass strip into 1cm/⅜in squares. Turn the strip over so the score lines face the worktop and tap each score line with the ball end of the glass cutter. The glass should break easily into squares.

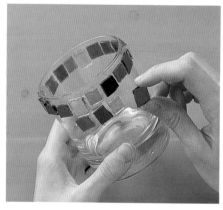

4 Using ultraviolet glue, stick the glass mosaic pieces around the glass tumbler, working from the top to the bottom. Leave a gap of 2mm/¹⁄₁₆in between squares to allow for grouting.

5 In a bowl, mix 30ml/2 tbsp of tile grout with 25ml/1½ tbsp of cold water and a 5cm/2in length of black acrylic paint. Stir until it forms a smooth, dark grey paste.

6 Using a spatula, press the grout into the gaps between the mosaic pieces. Remove any excess with the spatula, then allow to dry.

7 When the grout is dry, use a damp sponge scourer to clean any remaining smears of grout from the surface of the mosaic pieces.

8 When the lantern is clean, place a night-light in it. Never leave burning candles unattended and always keep them out of the reach of children.

Personal letters and correspondence often have a tendency to be lost or misplaced in a busy household. This simple design for a letter rack could be the solution.

Love Letter Rack

You will need

3mm/⅛in and 1.5cm/½in MDF
(medium-density fibreboard)
or plywood

pencil

jigsaw

PVA (white) glue

paintbrushes

wood glue

panel pins (narrow-headed nails)

pin hammer

vitreous glass tesserae

tile nippers

white cellulose filler

grout spreader or flexible knife

sponge

sandpaper

red acrylic paint

1 Draw the shapes of the components of the rack on to both pieces of MDF (medium-density fibreboard) or plywood. Cut them out with a jigsaw. Prime the surfaces with diluted PVA (white) glue. When dry, draw the pattern on to the front panel. Stick the pieces together with wood glue and secure with panel pins. Leave to dry overnight.

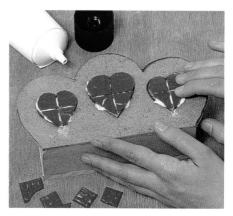

2 Select two tones of red vitreous glass tesserae to tile the heart motifs. Using tile nippers, nibble the tesserae into precise shapes to fit your design. Fix the tesserae in position on the front panel of the letter rack with white cellulose filler.

3 Select the colours of vitreous glass to tile around the hearts. Trim the tesserae to fit snugly around the heart motif and within the edges of the letter rack. Fix them to the base. Leave the rack to dry overnight.

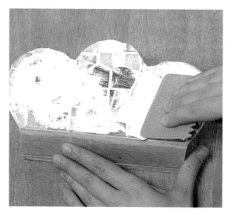

4 Smooth more filler over the mosaic using a grout spreader or flexible knife. Rub the filler into all of the gaps with your fingers. Rub off any excess filler with a damp sponge and leave to dry.

5 Use sandpaper to remove any filler that has dried on the surface of the mosaic and to neaten the edges. Paint the parts of the letter rack that are not covered with mosaic with red acrylic paint. Leave to dry.

A plain terracotta pot is decorated with squares of brightly coloured tesserae and mirror glass, set in white tile adhesive. This project is very simple to do – you could decorate several matching pots.

Jazzy Plant Pot

You will need

small terracotta plant pot
yacht varnish
paintbrush
vitreous glass tesserae
tile nippers
mirror glass
white cement-based tile adhesive
mixing bowl
flexible knife
sponge
sandpaper
soft cloth

1 Paint the inside of the plant pot with yacht varnish. Leave to dry. Cut the tesserae into neat quarters using tile nippers. Cut small squares of mirror glass the same size, also with tile nippers. Continue cutting the tesserae until you have enough pieces, in a variety of colours, to cover your pot completely.

2 Mix a quantity of tile adhesive as recommended by the manufacturer. Working from the bottom of the pot, spread a thick layer over a small area at a time using a flexible knife. Press the tesserae into the tile adhesive in rows, including the pieces of mirror glass. Leave to dry overnight.

3 Mix some more tile adhesive and rub all over the surface of the mosaic. Fill any gaps in between the tesserae, then wipe off excess adhesive with a damp sponge before it dries. Again, leave to dry overnight.

4 Use sandpaper to remove any lumps of tile adhesive that may have dried on to the surface of the tesserae, and to neaten the bottom edge of the pot.

5 Mix some more tile adhesive and smooth it all over the rim of the pot. Leave until completely dry, and then polish the finished mosaic well with a soft cloth.

This design relies on the various effects that are created by the juxtaposition of colours and textures. It can quite easily be adapted but should be kept simple for the best effect.

Mosaic Bottle

You will need
wine bottle
silicone sealant
pencil or pointed stick
vitreous glass tesserae, including white
tile nippers
cement-based tile adhesive
mixing container
soft cloth
sandpaper (optional)

1 Clean the bottle, rub off the label and dry thoroughly. Dab silicone sealant on to the bottle using a pencil or pointed stick to form a simple line drawing, such as a series of swirls.

2 Cut white vitreous glass into small pieces, about 2mm/¹⁄₁₆in and 4mm/¹⁄₈in, using tile nippers. Stick these tesserae to the lines drawn in silicone sealant, then leave overnight to dry.

3 Choose an assortment of colours from the vitreous glass and cut them into quarters. Some of the quarters will have to be cut across the diagonal, so that they can fit snugly between the white swirls. Stick these to the bottle in a series of bands of colour with the sealant. Leave overnight to dry.

4 Mix up some cement-based tile adhesive and rub the cement into the surface of the bottle. Make sure all the crevices between the tesserae are filled, otherwise the tesserae are liable to pull away, as the silicone sealant will remain rubbery. Wipe off excess cement with a dry soft cloth and leave overnight to dry.

5 If any of the tile adhesive has dried on to the surface of the tesserae, sand the bottle down. For a really smooth and glossy finish, polish the bottle with a dry soft cloth.

In this project, vitreous glass mosaic tiles in striking colours are used to decorate a ready-made fire screen. Most of this design uses whole tiles, cut diagonally into triangles.

Mosaic Fire Screen

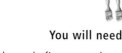

You will need

ready-made fire-screen base
pencil
ruler
sharp knife
PVA (white) glue
paintbrushes
vitreous glass tesserae
tile nippers
ready-mixed tile grout
nailbrush
wood primer
white undercoat
gloss paint
soft cloth

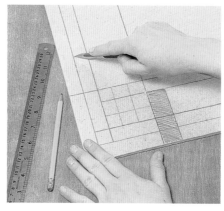

1 Draw the design on to the surface of the screen and its feet. Calculate the space needed to accommodate the tiles required and mark the main areas with a ruler. Score the whole of the surface with a sharp knife, then prime with diluted PVA (white) glue and leave to dry completely.

2 Select a range of vitreous glass tiles in the colours you require. Use tile nippers to cut some of the tiles into right-angled triangles to use for the inner border design.

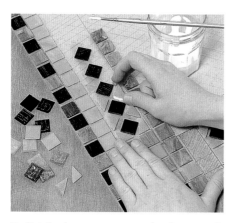

3 Stick the tesserae to the base with PVA glue. Try to make all the gaps between the tesserae equal and leave the area that will be slotted into the feet untiled.

4 Tile the edge, then the feet, making sure they will still slot on to the screen. Leave overnight to dry. Rub grout into the entire surface of the mosaic, making sure all the gaps between the tesserae are filled.

5 Leave the grout to dry for about ten minutes, then remove any excess with a nailbrush. Allow to dry for a further 12 hours, then paint the back of the screen with wood primer, then undercoat and finally gloss paint, allowing each coat to dry before you apply the next. Finally, polish the mosaic with a soft cloth and slot on the feet.

This mosaic jewellery box was inspired by the treasures of the Aztecs and Mayas of pre-Columbian Central America, which were decorated with turquoise, coral and jade.

Aztec Box

You will need

wooden box with hinged lid
felt-tipped pen or dark pencil
PVA (white) glue
glue brush
glass nuggets backed with gold and silver leaf
masking tape
fine artist's paintbrush
vitreous glass tesserae
tile nippers
cinca ceramic tiles
sand
cement
mixing container
black cement dye
sponge
soft cloth
plastic bag

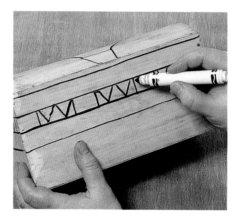

1 Draw the design on the wooden box with a felt-tipped pen or dark pencil. The design represents the head of a fierce animal, and the teeth and jaws of the beast are drawn immediately below the opening edge of the lid. Use the picture as a guide.

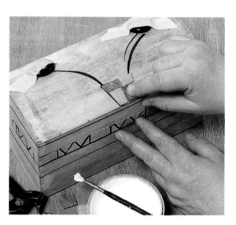

2 Using PVA (white) glue, stick glass nuggets on the box for the eyes. Hold them in place with masking tape to dry. Cut vitreous glass tiles in coral and stick on to the nose and lips. Cut vitreous glass tiles in terracotta and pink for the lips. Use a paintbrush to apply glue to small pieces.

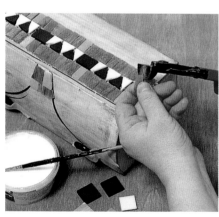

3 Cut triangular black and white tesserae into precise shapes to fit the areas marked for the teeth, then stick them in place.

4 Select tesserae in varying shades and use to define the eye sockets and the snout, cutting to fit as necessary. Include a few small nuggets positioned randomly. When tiling around the hinges, leave 1cm/½in untiled, so the box can be opened. Leave it to dry, then tile the lid in the same way.

5 Mix three parts sand with one part cement. Add some black cement dye. Add water, mixing it to the desired consistency. Rub the cement on to the box surface. Scrape off the excess, rub the box with a slightly damp sponge and polish with a dry cloth. Cover with plastic to dry slowly.

In this ambitious project the mosaic is arranged on a clear glass base. Place the screen in front of a window so that the light shines through, making the colours of the stained glass glow.

Stained-glass Screen

You will need

mitre block

hacksaw

tape measure

3 pieces of 2.5cm/1in x 3.5cm/1½in wood, each 206cm/81in long, with a 1cm/½in rebate

wood glue

hammer

12 corner staples

pencil

hand drill

4 small hinges

screwdriver and screws

large sheet of paper

indelible felt-tipped pen

3 pieces of clear glass, each 70 x 25cm/27½ x 10in

glass cutter

7 pieces of coloured glass, 27cm/10½in square

clear all-purpose adhesive

tile grout

universal black stain

mixing bowl

old toothbrush

paint scraper

soft cloths

3 pieces of rectangular beading, each 2m/79in long

panel pins (brads)

12 metal corner plates

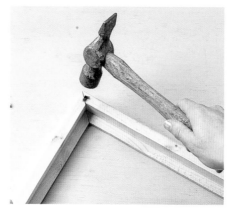

1 Using a mitre block and a hacksaw, cut two pieces of rebated wood 74cm/ 29in long, and two 29cm/11½in long from each length for the frame. Arrange the wood into three frames. Glue the mitred ends together with wood glue, checking that they are at right angles. Leave to dry, then hammer in a corner staple at each corner.

2 Place one frame on top of another, with the rebates facing outwards. With a pencil, mark the position of two small hinges and their screwholes on two adjacent side edges of the frames. Drill a shallow guidehole for each screw, then screw in the hinges. Attach the third frame in the same way.

3 Place the three frames face down on a sheet of paper. Using a felt-tipped pen, draw around the inner edge of each frame. Draw a design that flows in bands across the frames. Centre the pieces of clear glass over the drawing. Trace the design on to the glass.

4 Using a glass cutter, cut 12 right-angled triangles of coloured glass for the corners of the screen and set aside. Cut the rest randomly.

5 Using clear adhesive, glue the coloured glass pieces on to the clear glass panels. Work on a section of your design at a time, following each band across to the other panels. Leave to dry for 2 hours.

6 Mix the tile grout with the black stain and rub it over the surface of the mosaic. Use a toothbrush to fill all the gaps. Leave to dry for 1 hour.

7 When completely dry, clean off the excess grout. Residual, stubborn grout can be removed carefully with a paint scraper. Finish removing any smaller areas of grout with a soft cloth.

8 Glue one of the reserved right-angled triangles of coloured glass over the corner of the frame, at the front. Repeat with the other triangles on each corner of the frame.

9 Cut each piece of beading into two lengths each 71cm/28in and two lengths each 23cm/9in. Put the glass panels in the frames, slot the beading behind them and fix them in place with panel pins (brads).

10 Make shallow guideholes with a hand drill, then screw the corner plates to the back of each corner of the frame. Finally polish the surface of your mosaic screen with a soft cloth.

Give your bathroom a new lease of life with this colourful and original fish splashback. Beads clustered together make an original addition to mosaics, and are perfect for creating intricate shapes.

Fish Splashback

You will need

pencil

paper

piece of plywood to fit splashback area

carbon paper

vitreous glass tesserae in a variety of colours

wood glue

interior filler

mixing container

spoon

acrylic paints in a variety of colours

selection of beads including:

metallic bugle beads,

frosted and metallic square beads,

large round beads and mixed beads

tile nippers

tile grout

cloth

1 Sketch the design to fit the splashback on a large sheet of paper, keeping the shapes simple and bold. Use a sheet of carbon paper to transfer the design to the plywood by drawing firmly over all the lines using a pencil.

2 Apply the mosaic border. Lay out all the tiles first, alternating the colours. Then apply wood glue to the border, a small section at a time, positioning the tiles carefully on top of the glue as you work along.

3 Following the manufacturer's instructions, mix up a small amount of interior filler, then add some green acrylic paint to colour it.

4 Spread green filler thickly over the seaweed fronds, then carefully press in metallic green bugle beads. Fill in the fish fins using green filler and metallic green square beads. Make sure all the beads are on their sides so that the holes do not show.

5 Mix up another small amount of interior filler, this time colouring it with the orange acrylic paint. Spread filler thickly over the starfish and press in orange square frosted beads. Use some darker beads for shading.

6 Glue on a large bead for the fish eye using wood glue. Mix up some white filler and spread it thickly on to a 5cm/2in-square section of the fish body and press in mixed beads. Repeat, working in small sections, until the fish is complete.

7 Glue on large beads for bubbles. For the background design and the rocks at the bottom of the splashback, use mosaic tile nippers to cut the mosaic tiles into 1cm/½in squares.

8 Fill in the background, varying the shades and sticking the tiles down with wood glue. Clip the edges of the tiles to fit any curves. Mix up some tile grout following the manufacturer's instructions and spread over the design. Spread lightly and carefully over the beaded areas. Wipe off with a damp cloth and leave to dry.

This design is simple to execute and adds a naive charm to a plain wooden tray. The semi-indirect method of mosaic used here helps to keep the surface smooth and flat.

Country Cottage Tray

You will need

scissors
brown paper
wooden tray
pencil
tracing paper (optional)
tile nippers
vitreous glass tesserae
water-soluble glue
white spirit (paint thinner)
PVA (white) glue
mixing container
old household paintbrush
bradawl (with chisel edge) or
other sharp instrument
masking tape
cement-based tile adhesive
notched spreader
sponge
soft cloth

1 Cut a piece of brown paper to fit the bottom of the wooden tray. Draw a very simple picture in pencil or trace the template at the back of the book. Plan out the colour scheme for the picture and, using the tile nippers, cut all of the vitreous glass tesserae into quarters.

2 Position the tiles on to the paper to check your design before going any further. Once you are satisfied with the design, apply water-soluble glue on to the paper in small areas, and stick the tiles on face down. Take care to obscure any pencil marks. Trim the tiles to fit if necessary.

3 Prepare the bottom of the tray by removing any varnish or polish with white spirit (paint thinner). Prime with diluted PVA (white) glue, leave it to dry, then score it with a sharp instrument such as a bradawl. Protect the sides with masking tape.

4 Mix the tile adhesive according to the manufacturer's instructions. Spread an even layer over the bottom of the tray, using a notched spreader. Cover the tray completely and spread well into the corners.

5 Place the mosaic carefully in the freshly-applied tile adhesive, paper side up. Press down firmly over the whole surface, then leave for about 30 minutes. Moisten the paper with a damp sponge and peel off. Leave the tile adhesive to dry overnight.

6 Some parts of the mosaic may need to be grouted with extra tile adhesive. Leave it to dry, then clean off any of the adhesive that may have dried on the surface with a sponge. Remove the pieces of masking tape and then polish the mosaic with a soft cloth.

Create your own abstract mirror frame using the semi-indirect method. This design features a colourful mixture of shapes in varying sizes. Copy it or use it as a basis for your own creation.

Abstract Mirror

You will need

circular wooden board, 40cm/16in diameter, with a 5mm/¼in lip

pair of compasses

pencil

brown paper

scissors

circle of mirror glass, 20cm/8in diameter

black felt-tipped pen

masking tape

vitreous glass tesserae

tile nippers

water-soluble glue and brush

craft knife

tile grout

mixing container

sponge

cement-based tile adhesive

notched spreader

silicone-based adhesive

1 Draw a circle on brown paper 2mm/¹⁄₁₆ in smaller than the board using a pair of compasses, and cut it out. Place the mirror in the centre and draw around it in black pen. Divide the border into eight equal sections. Draw a design clearly in each section.

2 Place the mirror face down in the centre of the paper and attach it with a curl of masking tape. Cut all the tesserae to size with the tile nippers. Stick them face down on to the paper design, using water-soluble glue. Keep the gaps between the tesserae even.

3 When the tile design is complete, carefully lower the mosaic on to the board and attach the lip around the outside. Remove the mirror and cut away the brown paper underneath it using a craft knife.

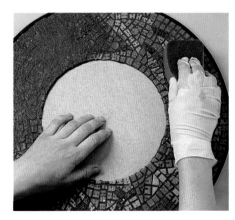

4 Rub a small amount of tile grout into the mosaic, then wipe off the excess with a damp sponge. This will bind the tesserae together. Leave it until the grout is almost dry.

5 Gently remove the mosaic from the board by turning the board upside down. Spread the outer area of the board with tile adhesive using a notched spreader. Press the mosaic into it firmly, tile side down.

6 Coat the back of the mirror with the silicone-based adhesive and stick it into the centre of the board. Leave to set for 20 minutes.

7 Dampen the paper with a sponge, wait 10 minutes, then gently peel it off the mosaic. Clean away any lumps of cement with a damp sponge. Leave to dry then re-grout the mosaic, filling in any cracks, and sponge clean.

This lovely mosaic table provides a stunning focal point for any room in the home. With its swirling pattern, the mosaic evokes fresh sea breezes sweeping in off the water.

Mosaic Table

You will need

piece of plywood

jigsaw

sharp knife

PVA (white) glue

paintbrushes

pencil

tile nippers

vitreous glass tesserae, in various colours

cement-based tile adhesive powder

soft brush

plastic spray bottle

cloths

fine sandpaper

1 Cut the plywood to the desired shape for your table. Score it with a sharp knife and prime it with a coat of diluted PVA (white) glue. Leave to dry thoroughly.

2 For the table design pictured here, use a pencil to draw a series of swirls radiating from the centre of the table. If you prefer, create your own design.

3 Use tile nippers to cut white glass tiles into quarters, and use different densities of white to add interest to the finished design.

4 Brush PVA glue along the pencil line swirls, then position the white glass tiles on top of the layer of glue, smooth side up.

5 Select your colours for the areas between the white lines. Here, browns and sand colours form the edge while blues, greens and whites are used for the central areas. Spread out your selected colours to see whether the combinations work.

6 Using the tile nippers, cut all of the coloured squares you have chosen into quarters.

7 Glue the central pieces to the table-top with PVA glue. To finish off the edge, glue pieces around the border of the table to match the design of the top surface. Leave the glue to dry thoroughly overnight.

8 Sprinkle dry cement-based tile adhesive over the mosaic and spread it with a brush, filling all the spaces. Spray with water wetting all of the cement. Wipe away any excess.

9 Mix up some tile adhesive with water and rub it into the edges of the table with your fingers. Leave it to dry overnight.

10 Rub off any excess cement with fine sandpaper and finish the table by polishing the mosaic thoroughly with a soft cloth.

This unusual garden urn is decorated with modern faces but has a look that is reminiscent of Byzantine icons. A simple and naive drawing of a face can look better than realistic depictions when rendered in mosaic.

Garden Urn

You will need

large frost-resistant urn

yacht varnish

paintbrush

chalk

vitreous glass tesserae

tile nippers

cement-based tile adhesive

mixing container

flexible knife

sponge

sandpaper

dilute hydrochloric acid (optional)

1 Paint the inside of the urn with yacht varnish, then leave to dry. Divide the pot into quarters and draw your design on each quarter with chalk. The design used here depicts four different heads and shoulders. Keep the drawing simple, sketching just the basic elements of the face.

2 Choose a dark colour from the range of tiles for the main outlines and details such as eyes and lips. Cut these into eighths using tile nippers. Mix up cement-based tile adhesive and stick the tesserae on to your drawn lines. Select a range of shades for the flesh tones and cut into quarters.

3 Working on a small area at a time, apply cement-based tile adhesive to the face and press the tesserae into it. Use a mixture of all the colours, but in areas of shade use more of the darker tesserae and in highlighted areas use more of the lighter pieces.

4 Choose colours for the area that surrounds the heads. Spread these out on a clean table to see if they work together. A mixture of blues and whites with a little green has been chosen here. Cut the pieces into quarters with tile nippers.

5 Working on a small area at a time, spread tile adhesive on to the surface and press the cut vitreous glass into it, making sure the colours are arranged randomly. Cover the outer surface of the urn with tesserae, then leave to dry for 24 hours.

6 Mix up more tile adhesive and spread it all over the surface of the mosaic. Do this thoroughly, making sure you fill all the gaps between the tesserae. This is especially important if the urn is going to be put outside. Wipe off any excess cement with a sponge and leave to dry for 24 hours.

7 Use sandpaper to remove any cement that has dried on the surface of the mosaic. If the cement is hard to remove, dilute hydrochloric acid can be used. Wear protective clothing and a mask. Wash any acid residue from the surface with plenty of water and leave the urn to dry.

8 Finish off the urn by rubbing some more of the tile adhesive over the lip and around the inside rim of the pot. This will prevent the mosaic design from seeming to end too abruptly and will give the urn and mosaic a more unified appearance.

Templates

Enlarge the templates on a photocopier. Alternatively, trace the design and draw a grid of evenly spaced squares over your tracing. Draw a larger grid on to another piece of paper and copy the outline square by square. Finally, draw over the lines to make sure they are continuous.

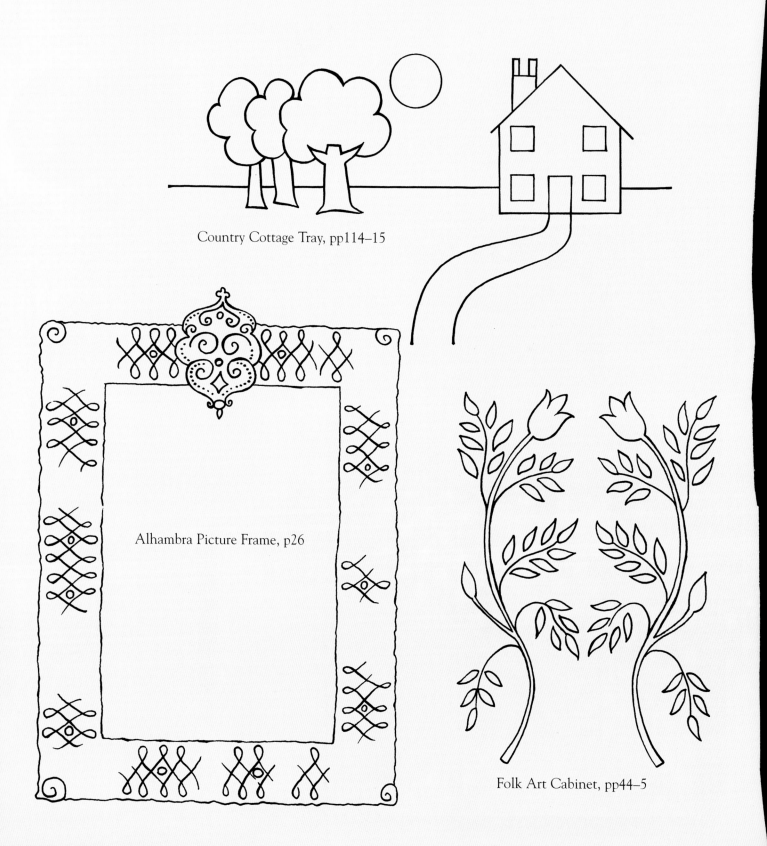

Country Cottage Tray, pp114–15

Alhambra Picture Frame, p26

Folk Art Cabinet, pp44–5

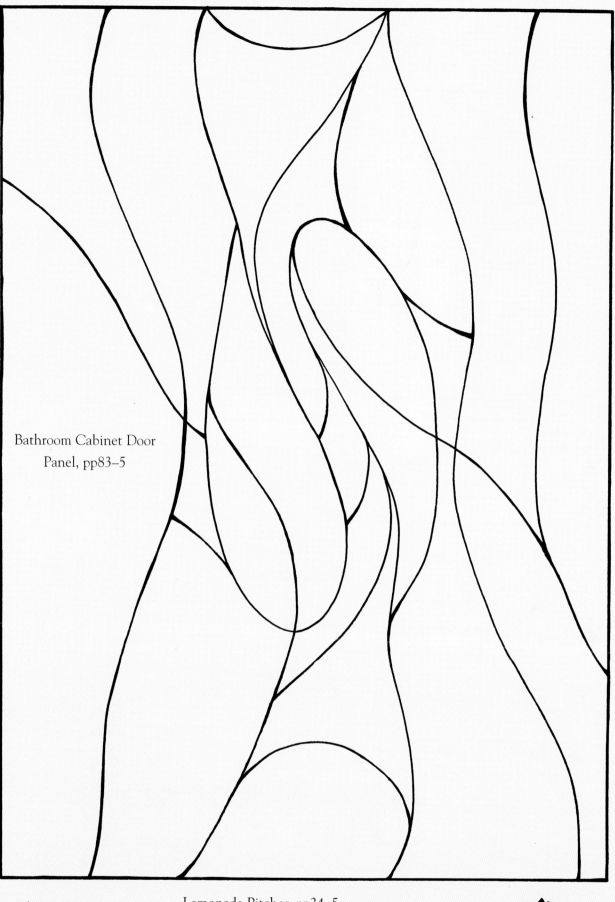

Bathroom Cabinet Door
Panel, pp83–5

Lemonade Pitcher, pp24–5

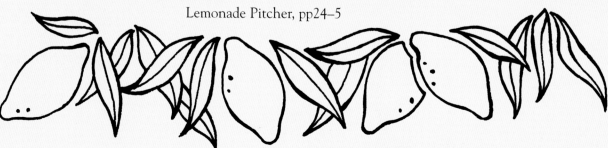

Venetian Perfume Bottle, pp42–3

Sunlight Catcher, pp22–3

Leaf Photograph Frame, pp20–1

Folk Art Glass, pp40–1

Bohemian Bottle, pp38–9

French-lavender Flower Vase, pp36–7

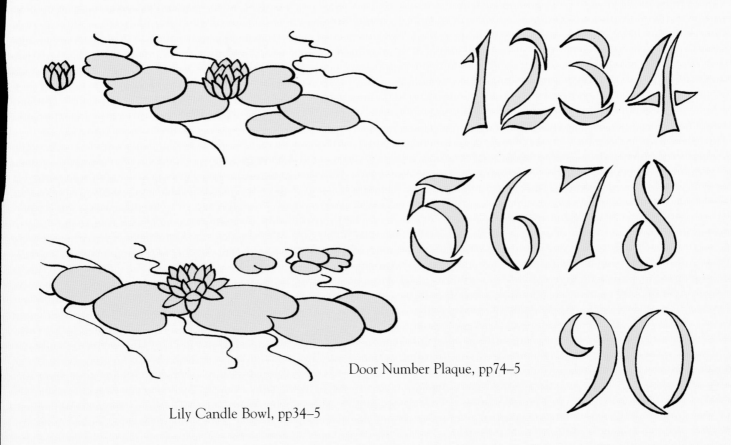

Door Number Plaque, pp74–5

Lily Candle Bowl, pp34–5

Indoor Glass Lantern, pp72–3

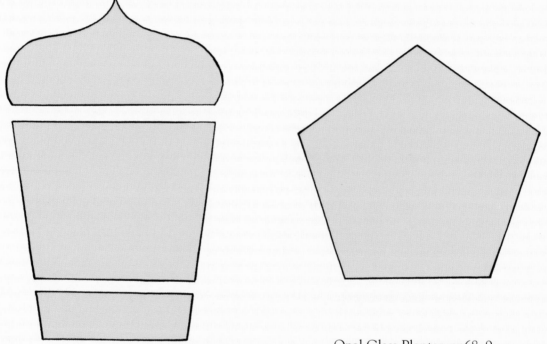

Opal Glass Planter, pp68–9

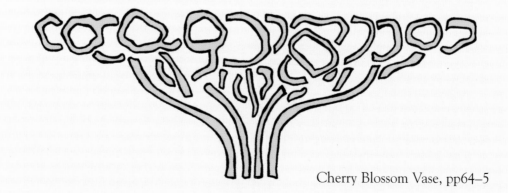

Cherry Blossom Vase, pp64–5

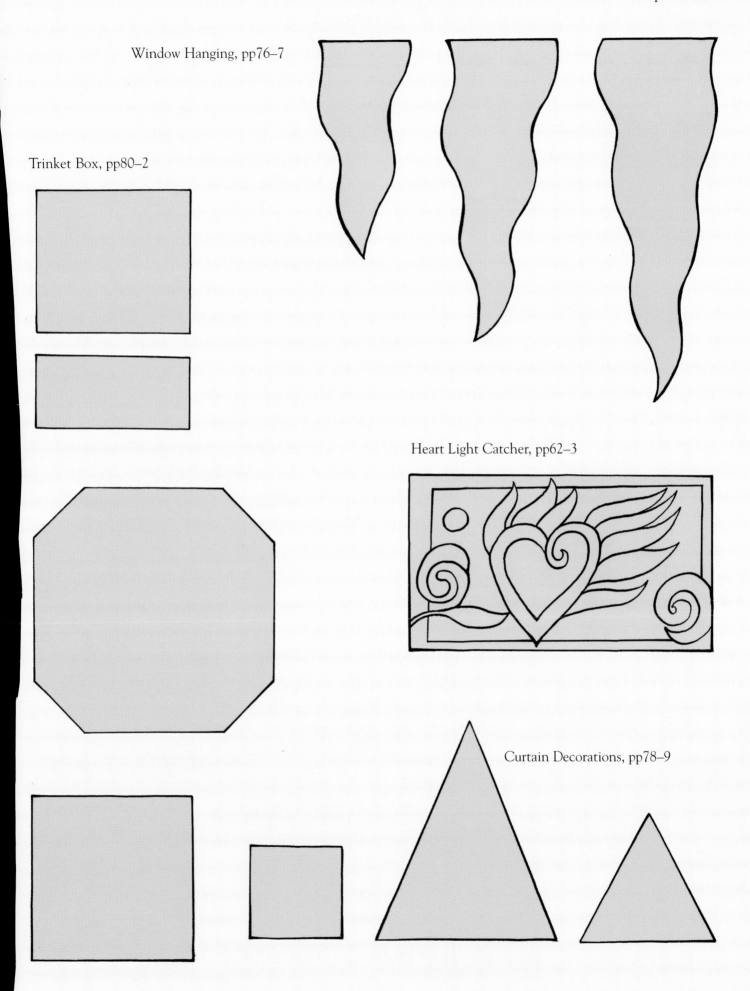

Window Hanging, pp76–7

Trinket Box, pp80–2

Heart Light Catcher, pp62–3

Curtain Decorations, pp78–9

Index